On Disobedience
and other essays

Other Books by Erich Fromm

Escape from Freedom
Man for Himself
The Sane Society
The Anatomy of Human Destructiveness

On Disobedience
and other essays

by Erich Fromm

The Seabury Press • New York

1981
The Seabury Press
815 Second Avenue
New York, N.Y. 10017

Printed in the United States of America

Library of Congress Cataloging in Publication Data

Fromm, Erich, 1900–1980
  On disobedience and other essays.

  1. Man—Addresses, essays, lectures. 2. Civilization,
Modern—1950- —Addresses, essays, lectures.
3. Alienation (Social psychology)—Addresses, essays,
lectures. I. Title.
BD450.F7825   128   81-2260
ISBN 0-8164-0500-X   AACR2

Contents

Foreword

Erich Fromm formulated in these essays what it means to be obedient to human nature and to the goal of a humane society, and to be disobedient to all sorts of idols and political ideologies. His reasoning is still relevant today. This disobedience to conformism and a critical stand against common "non-sense" should still be our main objective.

Fromm's psychological insights into social and political phenomena stimulated him to support for some time the American Socialist Party and to engage in the peace movement, as well as in steps toward disarmament. Here he practiced his disobedience to all forms of "common sense" and official political thinking, and his obedience to sane thinking as handed down by the prophets and demonstrated by such men as Albert Schweitzer and Bertrand Russell.

All the articles in this volume have been published before in books and magazines, but here they are brought together for the first time. They show Eric Fromm's deep concern and passion for peace and for mankind's survival.

I want to thank all who helped in the publication of this book.

Annis Fromm
Locarno, Switzerland, 1981

I. Values, Psychology and Human Existence

The thesis of this paper is that values are rooted in the very conditions of human existence; hence that our knowledge of these conditions—that is, of the "human situation"—leads us to establishing values which have objective validity; this validity exists only with regard to the existence of man; outside of him there are no values. What is the nature of man, what are the special conditions of human existence, and what are the needs which are rooted in these conditions?

Man is torn away from the primary union with nature, which characterizes animal existence. Having at the same time reason and imagination, he is aware of his aloneness and separateness, of his powerlessness and ignorance, of the accidentalness of his birth and of his death. He could not face this state of being for a second if he could not find new ties with his fellow man which replace the old ones, regulated by instincts. Even if all his physiological needs were satisfied, he would experience his state of aloneness and individuation as a prison from which he had to break out in order to retain his sanity. In fact, the insane person is the one who has completely failed to establish any kind of union and is imprisoned, even if he is not behind barred windows. The necessity to unite with other living beings, to be related to them, is an imperative need on which the fulfillment of man's sanity depends. This need is behind all phenomena which constitute the whole gamut of intimate human relations, of all passions which are called love in the broadest sense of the word.

There are several ways in which this union can be sought and achieved. Man can attempt to become one with the world by *submission* to a person, to a group, to an institution, to God. In this way he transcends the separateness of his individual existence by becoming part of somebody or something bigger than himself and experiences his identity in connection with the power to which he has submitted. Another possibility of overcoming separateness lies in the opposite direction: man can try to unite himself with the world by having *power* over it, by making others a part of himself, and thus transcending his individual existence by domination.

The common element in both submission and domination is the symbiotic nature of relatedness. Both persons involved have lost their integrity and freedom; they live on each other and from each other, satisfying their craving for closeness, yet suffering from the lack of inner strength and self-reliance which would require freedom and independence, and furthermore constantly threatened by the conscious or unconscious hostility which is bound to arise from the symbiotic relationship. The realization of the submissive (masochistic) or the domineering (sadistic) passion never leads to satisfaction. They have a self-propelling dynamism, and because no amount of submission or domination (or possession or fame) is enough to give a sense of identity and union, more and more of it is sought. The ultimate result of these passions is defeat. It cannot be otherwise; although these passions aim at the establishment of a sense of union, they destroy the sense of integrity. The person driven by any one of these passions actually becomes dependent on others; instead of developing his own individual being, he is dependent on those whom he submits to or whom he dominates.

There is only one passion which satisfies man's need to unite himself with the world and to acquire at the same time a sense of integrity and individuality, and this is *love. Love is union* with somebody, or something outside oneself *under the condition of retaining the separateness and integrity of one's own self.* It is an experience of sharing, of communion, which permits the full unfolding of one's own inner activity. The experience of love does away with the necessity of illusions. There is no need to inflate the image of the other person, or of myself, since the reality of active sharing and loving permits me to transcend my individualized existence and at the same time to experience myself as the bearer of the active powers which constitute the act of loving. What matters is the particular *quality* of loving, not the object. Love is in the experience of human solidarity with our fellow creatures, it is in the erotic love of man and woman, in the love of the mother for her child, and also in the love for oneself as a human being; it is in the mystical experience of union. In the act of loving, I am one with All, and yet I am myself, a unique, separate, limited, mortal human being. Indeed, out of the very polarity between separateness and union, love is born and reborn.

Another aspect of the human situation, closely connected with the need for relatedness, is man's situation as a *creature* and his need to *transcend* this very state of the passive creature. Man is thrown into this world without his consent or will. In this respect he is not different from the animal, from the plants, or from inorganic matter. But being endowed with reason and imagination, he cannot be content with the passive role of the creature, with the role of dice cast out of a cup. He is driven by the urge to transcend the role of the creature, the accidentalness and passivity of his existence, by becoming a "creator."

Man can create life. This is the miraculous quality which

he indeed shares with all living beings, but with the difference that he alone is aware of being created and of being a creator. Man can create life, or rather, woman can create life, by giving birth to a child and by caring for the child until it is sufficiently grown to take care of its own needs. Man—man and woman—can create by planting seeds, by producing material objects, by creating art, by creating ideas, by loving one another. In the act of creation man transcends himself as a creature, raises himself beyond the passivity and accidentalness of his existence into the realm of purposefulness and freedom. In man's need for transcendence lies one of the roots for love, as well as for art, religion, and material production.

To create presupposes activity and care. It presupposes love for that which one creates. How then does man solve the problem of transcending himself if he is not capable of creating, if he cannot love? *There is another answer to this need for transcendence; if I cannot create life, I can destroy it. To destroy life makes me also transcend it.* Indeed, that man can destroy life is just as miraculous a feat as that he can create it, for life is *the* miracle, the inexplicable. In the act of destruction, man sets himself above life; he transcends himself as a creature. Thus, the ultimate choice for man, inasmuch as he is driven to transcend himself, is to create or to destroy, to love or to hate. The enormous power of the will for destruction which we see in the history of man and which we have witnessed so frightfully in our own time is rooted in the nature of man, just as the drive to create is rooted in it. To say that man is capable of developing his primary potentiality for love and reason does not imply the naive belief in man's goodness. Destructiveness is a secondary potentiality, rooted in the very existence of man, and having the same intensity and power as any passion can have. But—and this is the essential point of my argument— it is the *alternative* to creativeness. Creation and destruction, love and hate, are not two instincts which exist independently. They are both answers to the same need for transcendence, and the will to destroy must rise when the will to create cannot be satisfied. However, the satisfaction of the need to create leads to happiness, destructiveness to suffering—most of all, for the destroyer himself.

A third need, again following the conditions of human existence, is that for *rootedness*. Man's birth as man means the beginning of his emergence from his natural home, the beginning of the severance of his natural ties. Yet this very severance is frightening; if man loses his natural roots, where is he and who is he? He would stand alone, without a home, without roots; he could not bear the isolation and helplessness of this position. He would become insane. He can dispense with the natural roots only insofar as he finds new *human* roots and only after he has found them can he feel at home again in this world. Is it surprising, then, to find a deep craving in man not to sever the natural ties, to fight against being torn away from nature, from mother, blood and soil?

The most elementary of the natural ties is the tie of the child to the mother. The child begins life in the mother's womb and exists there for a much longer time than is the case with most animals; even after birth, the child remains physically helpless and completely dependent on the mother; this period of helplessness and dependence again is much more protracted than with any animal. In the first years of life no full separation between child and mother has occurred. The satisfaction of all his physiological needs, of his vital need for warmth and affection depend on her; she has not only given birth to him, but she continues to give life to him. Her care is not dependent on anything the child does for her, on any obligation which the child has to fulfill; it is unconditional. She cares because the new creature is her child. The child, in these decisive first years of his life, has the experience of his mother as the fountain of life, as an all-enveloping, protective, nourishing power.

Mother is food; she is love; she is warmth; she is earth. To be loved by her means to be alive, to be rooted, to be at home.

Just as birth means to leave the enveloping protection of the womb, growing up means to leave the protective orbit of the mother. Yet, even in the mature adult, the longing for this situation as it once existed never ceases completely, in spite of the fact that there is, indeed, a great difference between the adult and the child. The adult has the means to stand on his own feet, to take care of himself and even for others, whereas the child is not yet capable of doing all this. But, considering the increased perplexities of life, the fragmentary nature of our knowledge, the accidentalness of adult existence, the unavoidable errors we make, the situation of the adult is by no means as different from that of the child as it is generally assumed. Every adult is in need of help, of warmth, of protection, in many ways differing and yet in many ways similar to the needs of the child. Is it surprising to find in the average adult a deep longing for the security and rootedness which the relationship to his mother once gave him? Is it not to be expected that he cannot give up this intense longing unless he finds other ways of being rooted?

In psychopathology we find ample evidence for this phenomenon of the refusal to leave the all-enveloping orbit of the mother. In the most extreme form we find the craving to return to the womb. A person obsessed by this desire may offer the picture of schizophrenia. He feels and acts like the fetus in the mother's womb, incapable of assuming even the most elementary functions of a small child. In many of the more severe neuroses we find the same craving, but as a repressed desire, manifested only in dreams, symptoms, and neurotic behavior, which results from the conflict between the deep desire to stay in the mother's womb and the adult part of the personality which tends to live a normal life. In dreams this craving appears in such symbols as being in a dark cave, in a one-man submarine, diving into deep water, etc. In the behavior of such a person, we find a fear of life and a deep fascination for death (death, in fantasy, being the return to the womb, to mother earth).

The less severe form of the fixation to mother is to be found in those cases where a person has permitted himself to be born, as it were, but where he is afraid to take the next step of birth, to be weaned from mother's breasts. People who have become arrested at this stage of birth have a deep craving to be mothered, nursed, protected by a motherly figure; they are the eternally dependent ones, who are frightened and insecure when motherly protection is withdrawn but optimistic and active when a loving mother or mother substitute is provided, either realistically or in fantasy.

Living is a process of continuous birth. The tragedy in the life of most of us is that we die before we are fully born. Being born, however, does not only mean to be free *from* the womb, the lap, the hand, etc., but also to be free *to* be active and creative. Just as the infant must breathe once the umbilical cord is cut, so man must be active and creative at every moment of birth. To the extent that man is fully born, he finds a new kind of rootedness; that lies in his creative relatedness to the world, and in the ensuing experience of solidarity with all man and with all nature. From being *passively* rooted in nature and in the womb, man becomes one again—but this time actively and creatively with all life.

Fourth, man needs to have a *sense of identity*. Man can be defined as the animal that can say "I," that can be aware of himself as a separate entity. The animal, being within nature and not transcending it, has no awareness of himself, has no need for a sense of identity. Man, being torn away from nature, being endowed with reason and imagination, needs to form a concept of himself, needs to say and to feel "I am I." Because he is not *lived*, but *lives*, because he has lost the original unity with nature, has to make decisions, is aware of himself and of his neighbor as different persons, he must be able to sense himself as the subject of his actions. As with the need for relatedness, rootedness, and transcendence, this need for a sense of identity is so vital and imperative that man could not remain sane if he did not find some way of satisfying it. Man's sense of identity develops in the process of emerging from the "primary bonds" which tie him to mother and nature. The infant still feeling one with mother, cannot yet say "I," nor has he any need for it. Only after he has conceived of the outer world as being separate and different from himself does he come to the awareness of himself as a distinct being, and one of the last words he learns to use is "I," in reference to himself.

In the development of *the human race* the degree to which man is aware of himself as a separate self depends on the extent to which he has emerged from the clan and the extent to which the process of individuation has developed. The member of a primitive clan might express his sense of identity in the formula "I am we"; he cannot yet conceive of himself as an "individual," existing apart from his group. In the medieval world, the individual was identified with his social role in the feudal hierarchy. The peasant was not a man who happened to be a peasant, the feudal lord not a man who happened to be a feudal lord. *He was* a peasant or a lord, and this sense of his unalterable station was an essential part of his sense of identity. When the feudal system broke down, this sense of identity was shaken and the acute question "Who am I?"—or, more precisely, "How do I know that I am I?"—arose. This is the question that was raised, in a philosophical form, by René Descartes. He answered the quest for identity by saying, "I doubt, hence I think; I think, hence I am." This answer put all the emphasis on the experience of "I" as the subject of my *thinking* activity, and failed to see that the "I" is experienced also in the process of feeling and creative action.

The development of Western culture went in the direction of creating the basis for the full experience of individuality. By making the individual free politically and economically, by teaching him to think for himself and freeing him from an authoritarian pressure, one hoped to enable him to feel "I" in the sense that he was the center and active subject of his powers and experienced himself as such. But only a minority achieved the new experience of "I." For the majority, individualism was not much more than a facade behind which was hidden the failure to acquire an individual sense of identity.

Many substitutes for a truly individual sense of identity were sought for and found. Nation, religion, class, and occupation serve to furnish a sense of identity. "I am an American." "I am a Protestant." "I am a businessman." These are the formulae that help a man experience a sense of identity after the original clan identity has disappeared and before a truly individual sense of identity has been acquired. These different identifications are, in contemporary society, usually employed together. They are in a broad sense status identifications, and they are more efficient if blended with older feudal remnants, as in European countries. In the United States, where so little is left of feudal relics and where there is so much social mobility, these status identifications are naturally less efficient, and the sense of identity is shifted more and more to the experience of conformity.

Inasmuch as I am not different, inasmuch as I am like the others and recognized by them as "a regular fellow," I can sense myself as "I." I am "as you desire me"—as Pirandello put it in the title of one of his plays. Instead of the pre-individualistic clan identity, a new herd identity develops in which the sense of identity rests on the sense of an unquestionable belonging to the crowd. That this uniformity and conformity are often not recognized as such, and are covered by the illusion of individuality, does not alter the facts.

The problem of the sense of identity is not, as it is usually understood, merely a philosophical problem, or a problem concerning only our mind and thought. The need to feel a sense of identity stems from the very condition of human existence, and it is the source of the most intense strivings. Since I cannot remain sane without the sense of "I," I am driven to do almost anything to acquire this sense. Behind the intense passion for status and conformity is this very need, and it is sometimes even stronger than the need for physical survival. What could be more obvious than the fact that people are willing to risk their lives, to give up their love, to surrender their freedom, to sacrifice their own thoughts for the sake of being one of the herd, of conforming, and thus of acquiring a sense of identity, even though it is an illusory one.

The fact that man has reason and imagination leads to the necessity not only for having a sense of his own identity but also for *orienting himself in the world intellectually*. This need can be compared with the process of physical orientation that develops in the first years of life and that is completed when the child can walk by himself, touch and handle things, knowing what they are. But when the ability to walk and to speak has been acquired, only the first step in the direction of orientation has been taken. Man finds himself surrounded by many puzzling phenomena and, having reason, he has to make sense of them, has to put them in some context which he can understand and which permits him to deal with them in his thoughts. The further his reason develops, the more adequate becomes his system of orientation, that is, the more it approximates reality. But even if man's frame of orientation is utterly illusory, it satisfies his need for some picture which is meaningful to him. Whether he believes in the power of a totem animal, in a rain god, or in the superiority and destiny of his race, his need for some frame of orientation is satisfied. Quite obviously, the picture of the world that he has depends on the development of his reason and of his knowledge. Although biologically the brain capacity of the human race has remained the same for thousands of generations, it takes a long evolutionary process to arrive at *objectivity*, that is, to acquire the faculty to see the world, nature, other persons, and oneself as they are and not distorted by desires and fears. The more man develops this objectivity, the more he is in touch with reality, the more he matures, the better can he create a human world in which he is at home. Reason is man's faculty for *grasping* the world by thought, in contradiction to intelligence, which is man's ability to *manipulate* the world with the help of thought. Reason is man's instrument for arriving at the truth, intelligence is man's instrument for manipulating the world more successfully; the former is essentially human, the latter belongs also to the animal part of man.

Reason is a faculty which must be practiced in order to develop, and it is indivisible. By this I mean that the faculty for objectivity refers to the knowledge of nature as well as to the knowledge of man, of society, and of oneself. If one lives in illusions about one sector of life, one's capacity for reason is restricted or damaged, and thus the use of reason is inhibited with regard to all other sectors. Reason in this respect is like love. Just as love is an orientation which refers to all objects and is incompatible with the restriction to one object, so is reason a human faculty which must embrace the whole of the world with which man is confronted.

The need for a frame of orientation exists on two levels; the first and the more fundamental need is to have *some* frame of orientation, regardless of whether it is true or false. Unless man has such a subjectively satisfactory frame of orientation, he cannot live sanely. On the second level, the need is to be in touch with reality by reason, to grasp the world objectively. But the necessity to develop his reason is not as immediate as that to develop some frame of orientation, since what is at stake for man in the latter case is his happiness and serenity, and not his sanity. This becomes clear if we study the function of *rationalization*. However unreasonable or immoral an action may be, man has an insuperable urge to rationalize it, that is, to prove to himself and to others that his action is determined by intelligence, common sense, or at least conventional morality. He has little difficulty in acting irrationally, but it is almost impossible for him not to give his action the appearance of reasonable motivation.

If man were only a disembodied intellect, his aim would be achieved by a comprehensive thought system. But since he is an entity endowed with a body as well as a mind, he has to react to the dichotomy of his existence not only in thinking but in the total process of living, in his feelings and actions. Hence any satisfying system of orientation contains not only intellectual elements but elements of feeling and sensing which are expressed in the relationship to an object of devotion.

The answers given to man's need for a system of orientation and an object of devotion differ widely both in content and in form. There are primitive systems such as animism and totemism in which natural objects or ancestors represent answers to man's quest for meaning. There are nontheistic systems, such as Buddhism, which are usually called religions although in their original form there is no concept of God. There are purely philosophical systems, such as Stoicism, and there are the monotheistic religious systems that give an answer to man's quest for meaning in reference to the concept of God.

But whatever their contents, they all respond to man's need to have not only some thought system but also an object of devotion that gives meaning to his existence and to his position in the world. Only the analysis of the various forms of religion can show which answers are better and which are worse solutions to man's quest for meaning and devotion, "better" or "worse" always considered from the standpoint of man's nature and his development.

In discussing the various needs of man as they result from the conditions of his existence, I have tried to indicate that they have to be satisfied in some way or other lest man should become insane. But there are several ways in which each of these needs can be satisfied; the difference between these ways is the difference in their appropriateness for the development of man. The need to be related can be satisfied by submission or by domination; but only in love is another human need fulfilled—that of independence and integrity of the self. The need for transcendence can be satisfied either by creativeness or by destructiveness; but only creativeness permits of joy, whereas destructiveness causes suffering for oneself and others. The need for rootedness can be satisfied regressively by fixation in nature and mother, or progressively by full birth in which new solidarity and oneness is achieved. Here again only in the latter case are individuality and integrity preserved. A frame of orientation may be irrational or rational; yet only the rational one can serve as a basis for the growth and development of the total personality. Eventually, the sense of identity can be based on primary ties with nature and clan, on adjustment to a group, or, on the other hand, on the full, creative development of the person. Again, only in the latter case can man achieve a sense of joy and strength.

The difference between the various answers is the difference between mental health and mental sickness, between suffering and joy, between stagnation and growth, between life and death, between good and evil. All answers that can be qualified as good have in common that they are consistent with the very nature of life, which is continuous birth and growth. All answers that can be qualified as bad have in common that they conflict with the nature of life, that they are conducive to stagnation and eventually to death. Indeed, at the moment man is born, life asks him a question, the question of human existence. He must answer this question at every moment of his life. *He* must answer it, not his mind, or his body, but *he*, the real person, his feet, his hands, his eyes, his stomach, his mind, his feeling, his real—not an imagined or abstracted—person. There are only a limited number of answers to the question of existence. We find these answers in the history of religion, from the most primitive to the highest. We find them also in the variety of characters, from the fullest sanity to the deepest psychosis.

In the foregoing remarks I have tried to outline these various answers, implying that each individual represents in himself the whole of humanity and its evolution. We find individuals who represent man on the most primitive level of history, and others who represent mankind as it will be thousands of years from now.

I said that the answer to life that corresponds to the reality of human existence is conducive to mental health. What is generally understood by mental health, however, is negative, rather than positive; the *absence of sickness, rather than the presence of well-being.* Actually there is even very little discussion in the psychiatric and psychological literature of what constitutes well-being.

I would describe well-being as the *ability to be creative, to be aware, and to respond;* to be independent and fully active, and by this very fact to be one with the world. To be concerned with *being,* not with *having;* to experience joy in the very act of living, and to consider living creatively as the only meaning of life. Well-being is not an assumption in the *mind* of a person. It is expressed in his whole body, in the way he walks, talks, in the tonus of his muscles.

Certainly, anyone who wants to achieve this aim must struggle against many basic trends of modern culture. I want to mention very briefly only two. One, the idea of a *split between intellect and affect,* an idea which has been prevalent from Descartes to Freud. In this whole development (to which there are, of course, exceptions) the assumption is made that only the intellect is rational and that affect, by its very nature, is irrational. Freud has made this assumption very explicitly by saying that love by its very nature is neurotic, infantile, irrational. His aim was actually to help man succeed in dominating irrational affect by intellect; or, to put it into his own words, "Where there was Id, there shall be Ego." Yet this dogma of the split between affect and thought does not correspond to the reality of human existence, and is destructive of human growth. We cannot understand man fully nor achieve the aim of well-being unless we overcome the idea of this split, restore to man his original unity, and recognize that the split between affect and thought, body and mind, is nothing but a product of our own thought and does not correspond to the reality of man.

The other obstacle to the achievement of well-being, deeply rooted in the spirit of modern society, is the fact of man's dethronement from his supreme place. The nineteenth century said "God is dead"; the twentieth century could say "Man is dead." Means have been transformed into ends, the production and consumption of things has become the aim of life, to which living is subordinated. We produce things that act like men and men that act like things. Man has transformed himself into a thing and worships the products of his own hands; he is alienated from himself and has regressed to idolatry, even though he uses God's name. Emerson already saw that "things are in the saddle and ride mankind." Today many of us see it. The achievement of well-being is possible only under one condition: *if we put man back into the saddle.*

II.   Disobedience as a Psychological and Moral Problem

For centuries kings, priests, feudal lords, industrial bosses and parents have insisted that *obedience is a virtue* and that *disobedience is a vice*. In order to introduce another point of view, let us set against this position the following statement: *human history began with an act of disobedience, and it is not unlikely that it will be terminated by an act of obedience.*

Human history was ushered in by an act of disobedience according to the Hebrew and Greek myths. Adam and Eve, living in the Garden of Eden, were part of nature; they were in harmony with it, yet did not transcend it. They were in nature as the fetus is in the womb of the mother. They were human, and at the same time not yet human. All this changed when they disobeyed an order. By breaking the ties with earth and mother, by cutting the umbilical cord, man emerged from a pre-human harmony and was able to take the first step into independence and freedom. The act of disobedience set Adam and Eve free and opened their eyes. They recognized each other as strangers and the world outside them as strange and even hostile. Their act of disobedience broke the primary bond with nature and made them individuals. "Original sin," far from corrupting man, set him free; it was the beginning of history. Man had to leave the Garden of Eden in order to learn to rely on his own powers and to become fully human.

The prophets, in their messianic concept, confirmed the idea that man had been right in disobeying; that he had not been corrupted by his "sin," but freed from the fetters of pre-human harmony. For the prophets, *history* is the place where man becomes human; during its unfolding he develops his powers of reason and of love until he creates a new harmony between himself, his fellow man and nature. This new harmony is described as "the end of days," that period of history in which there is peace between man and man, and between man and nature. It is a "new" paradise created by man himself, and one which he alone could create because he was forced to leave the "old" paradise as a result of his disobedience.

Just as the Hebrew myth of Adam and Eve, so the Greek myth of Prometheus sees all of human civilization based on an act of disobedience. Prometheus, in stealing the fire from the gods, lays the foundation for the evolution of man. There would be no human history were it not for Prometheus' "crime." He, like Adam and Eve, is punished for his disobedience. But he does not repent and ask for forgiveness. On the contrary, he proudly says: "I would rather be chained to this rock than be the obedient servant of the gods."

Man has continued to evolve by acts of disobedience. Not only was his spiritual development possible only because there were men who dared to say no to the powers that be in the name of their conscience or their faith, but also his intellectual development was dependent on the capacity for being disobedient—disobedient to authorities who tried to muzzle new thoughts and to the authority of long-established opinions which declared a change to be nonsense.

If the capacity for disobedience constituted the beginning of human history, obedience might very well, as I have said, cause the end of human history. I am not speaking symbolically or poetically. There is the possibility, or even the probability, that the human race will destroy civilization and even all life upon earth within the next five to ten years. There is no rationality or sense in it. But the fact is that, while we are living technically in the Atomic Age, the majority of men—including most of those who are in power—still live emotionally in the Stone Age; that while our mathematics, astronomy, and the natural sciences are of the twentieth century, most of our ideas about politics, the state, and society lag far behind the age of science. If mankind commits suicide it will be because people will obey those who command them to push the deadly buttons; because they will obey the archaic passions of fear, hate, and greed; because they will obey obsolete clichés of State sovereignty and national honor. The Soviet leaders talk much about revolutions, and we in the "free world" talk much about freedom. Yet they and we discourage disobedience—in the Soviet Union explicitly and by force, in the free world implicitly and by the more subtle methods of persuasion.

But I do not mean to say that all disobedience is a virtue and all obedience a vice. Such a view would ignore the dialectical relationship between obedience and disobedience. Whenever the principles which are obeyed and those which are disobeyed are irreconcilable, an act of obedience to one principle is necessarily an act of disobedience to its counterpart, and vice versa. Antigone is the classic example of this dichotomy. By obeying the inhuman laws of the State, Antigone necessarily would disobey the laws of humanity. By obeying the latter, she must disobey the former. All martyrs of religious faiths, of freedom and of science have had to disobey those who wanted to muzzle them in order to obey their own consciences, the laws of humanity and of reason. If a man can only obey and not disobey, he is a slave; if he can only disobey and not obey, he is a rebel (not a revolutionary); he acts out of anger, disappointment, resentment, yet not in the name of a conviction or a principle.

However, in order to prevent a confusion of terms an important qualification must be made. Obedience to a person, institution or power (heteronomous obedience) is submission; it implies the abdication of my autonomy and the acceptance of a foreign will or judgment in place of my own. Obedience to my own reason or conviction (autonomous obedience) is not an act of submission but one of affirmation. My conviction and my judgment, if authentically mine, are part of me. If I follow them rather than the judgment of others, I am being myself; hence the word *obey* can be applied only in a metaphorical sense and with a meaning which is fundamentally different from the one in the case of "heteronomous obedience."

But this distinction still needs two further qualifications, one with regard to the concept of conscience and the other with regard to the concept of authority.

The word *conscience* is used to express two phenomena which are quite distinct from each other. One is the "authoritarian conscience" which is the internalized voice of an authority whom we are eager to please and afraid of displeasing. This authoritarian conscience is what most people experience when they obey their conscience. It is also the conscience which Freud speaks of, and which he called "Super-Ego." This Super-Ego represents the internalized commands and prohibitions of father, accepted by the son out of fear. Different from the authoritarian conscience is the "humanistic conscience"; this is the voice present in every human being and independent from external sanctions and rewards. Humanistic conscience is based on the fact that as human beings we have an intuitive knowledge of what is human and inhuman, what is conducive of life and what is destructive of life. This conscience serves our functioning as human beings. It is the voice which calls us back to ourselves, to our humanity.

Authoritarian conscience (Super-Ego) is still obedience to

a power outside of myself, even though this power has been internalized. Consciously I believe that I am following *my* conscience; in effect, however, I have swallowed the principles of *power;* just because of the illusion that humanistic conscience and Super-Ego are identical, internalized authority is so much more effective than the authority which is clearly experienced as not being part of me. Obedience to the "authoritarian conscience," like all obedience to outside thoughts and power, tends to debilitate "humanistic conscience," the ability to be and to judge oneself.

The statement, on the other hand, that obedience to another person is *ipso facto* submission needs also to be qualified by distinguishing "irrational" from "rational" authority. An example of rational authority is to be found in the relationship between student and teacher; one of irrational authority in the relationship between slave and master. Both relationships are based on the fact that the authority of the person in command is accepted. Dynamically, however, they are of a different nature. The interests of the teacher and the student, in the ideal case, lie in the same direction. The teacher is satisfied if he succeeds in furthering the student; if he has failed to do so, the failure is his and the student's. The slave owner, on the other hand, wants to exploit the slave as much as possible. The more he gets out of him the more satisfied he is. At the same time, the slave tries to defend as best he can his claims for a minimum of happiness. The interests of slave and master are antagonistic, because what is advantageous to the one is detrimental to the other. The superiority of the one over the other has a different function in each case; in the first it is the condition for the furtherance of the person subjected to the authority, and in the second it is the condition for his exploitation. Another distinction runs parallel to this: rational authority is rational because the authority, whether it is held by a teacher or a captain of a ship giving orders in an emergency, acts in the name of reason which, being universal, I can accept without submitting. Irrational authority has to use force or suggestion, because no one would let himself be exploited if he were free to prevent it.

Why is man so prone to obey and why is it so difficult for him to disobey? As long as I am obedient to the power of the State, the Church, or public opinion, I feel safe and protected. In fact it makes little difference what power it is that I am obedient to. It is always an institution, or men, who use force in one form or another and who fraudulently claim omniscience and omnipotence. My obedience makes me part of the power I worship, and hence I feel strong. I can make no error, since it decides for me; I cannot be alone, because it watches over me; I cannot commit a sin, because it does not let me do so, and even if I do sin, the punishment is only the way of returning to the almighty power.

In order to disobey, one must have the courage to be alone, to err and to sin. But courage is not enough. The capacity for courage depends on a person's state of development. Only if a person has emerged from mother's lap and father's commands, only if he has emerged as a fully developed individual and thus has acquired the capacity to think and feel for himself, only then can he have the courage to say "no" to power, to disobey.

A person can become free through acts of disobedience by learning to say no to power. But not only is the capacity for disobedience the condition for freedom; freedom is also the condition for disobedience. If I am afraid of freedom, I cannot dare to say "no," I cannot have the courage to be disobedient. Indeed, freedom and the capacity for disobedience are inseparable; hence any social, political, and religious system which proclaims freedom, yet stamps out disobedience, cannot speak the truth.

There is another reason why it is so difficult to dare to disobey, to say "no" to power. During most of human history obedience has been identified with virtue and disobedience with sin. The reason is simple: thus far throughout most of history a minority has ruled over the majority. This rule was made necessary by the fact that there was only enough of the good things of life for the few, and only the crumbs remained for the many. If the few wanted to enjoy the good things and, beyond that, to have the many serve them and work for them, one condition was necessary: the many had to learn obedience. To be sure, obedience can be established by sheer force. But this method has many disadvantages. It constitutes a constant threat that one day the many might have the means to overthrow the few by force; furthermore there are many kinds of work which cannot be done properly if nothing but fear is behind the obedience. Hence the obedience which is only rooted in the fear of force must be transformed into one rooted in man's heart. Man must want and even need to obey, instead of only fearing to disobey. If this is to be achieved, power must assume the qualities of the All Good, of the All Wise; it must become All Knowing. If this happens, power can proclaim that disobedience is sin and obedience virtue; and once this has been proclaimed, the many can accept obedience because it is good and detest disobedience because it is bad, rather than to detest themselves for being cowards. From Luther to the nineteenth century one was concerned with overt and explicit authorities. Luther, the pope, the princes, wanted to uphold it; the middle class, the workers, the philosophers, tried to uproot it. The fight against authority in the State as well as in the family was often the very basis for the development of an independent and daring person. The fight against authority was inseparable from the intellectual mood which characterized the philosophers of the enlightenment and the scientists. This "critical mood" was one of faith in reason, and at the same time of doubt in everything which is said or thought, inasmuch as it is based on tradition, superstition, custom, power. The principles *sapere aude* and *de omnibus est dubitandum*—"dare to be wise" and "of all one must doubt"—were characteristic of the attitude which permitted and furthered the capacity to say "no."

The case of Adolf Eichmann is symbolic of our situation and has a significance far beyond the one which his accusers in the courtroom in Jerusalem were concerned with. Eichmann is a symbol of the organization man, of the alienated bureaucrat for whom men, women and children have become numbers. He is a symbol of all of us. We can see ourselves in Eichmann. But the most frightening thing about him is that after the entire story was told in terms of his own admissions, he was able in perfect good faith to plead his innocence. It is clear that if he were once more in the same situation he would do it again. And so would we—and so do we.

The organization man has lost the capacity to disobey, he is not even aware of the fact that he obeys. At this point in history the capacity to doubt, to criticize and to disobey may be all that stands between a future for mankind and the end of civilization.

III. The Application of Humanist Psychoanalysis to Marx's Theory

Marxism is humanism, and its aim is the full unfolding of man's potentialities—not man as deduced from his ideas or his consciousness, but man with his physical and psychic properties, the real man who does not live in a vacuum but in a social context, the man who has to produce in order to live. It is precisely the fact that the whole man, as well as his consciousness, is the concern of Marxist thought which differentiates Marx's "materialism" from Hegel's idealism, as well as from the economistic-mechanistic deformation of Marxism. It was Marx's great achievement to liberate the economic and philosophical categories that referred to man from their abstract and alienated expressions and to apply philosophy and economics *ad hominem*. Marx's concern was man, and his aim was man's liberation from the predomination of material interests, from the prison his own arrangements and deeds had built around him. If one does not understand this concern of Marx one will never understand either his theory or the falsification of it by many who claim to practice it. Even though Marx's main work is entitled *Capital* (*Das Kapital*), this work was meant to be only a step in his total research, to be followed by a history of philosophy. For Marx the study of capital was a critical tool to be used for understanding man's crippled state in industrial society. It is one step in the great work which, if he had been able to write it, might have been entitled *On Man and Society.*

Marx's work, that of the "young" Marx as well as that of the author of *Capital,* is full of psychological concepts. He deals with concepts like the "essence of man," and the "crippled man," with "alienation," with "consciousness," with "passionate strivings," and with "independence," to name only some of the most important. Yet, in contrast to Aristotle and Spinoza, who based ethics on a systematic psychology, Marx's work contains almost no psychological theory. Aside from fragmentary remarks on the distinction between fixed drives (like hunger and sexuality) and flexible drives which are socially produced, there is hardly any relevant psychology to be found in Marx's writings or, for that matter, in those of his successors. The reason for this failure does not lie in a lack of interest in or talent for analyzing psychological phenomena (the volumes containing the unabridged correspondence between Marx and Engels show a capacity for penetrating analysis of unconscious motivations that would be a credit to any gifted psychoanalyst); it is to be found in the fact that during Marx's lifetime there was no dynamic psychology that he could have applied to the problems of man. Marx died in 1883; Freud began to publish his work more than ten years after Marx's death.

The kind of psychology necessary to supplement Marx's analysis was, even though in need of many revisions, that created by Freud. Psychoanalysis is, first of all, a *dynamic* psychology. It deals with psychic *forces,* which motivate human behavior, action, feelings, ideas. These forces cannot always be seen as such; they have to be inferred from the observable phenomena, and to be studied in their contradictions and transformations. To be useful for Marxist thinking, a psychology must also be one which sees the *evolution* of these psychic forces as a process of constant interaction between man's needs and the social and historical reality in which he participates. It must be a psychology which is from the very beginning social psychology. Eventually, it must be a *critical* psychology, particularly one critical of man's consciousness.

Freud's psychoanalysis fulfills these main conditions, even though their relevance for Marxist thought was grasped neither by most Freudians nor by Marxists. The reasons for this failure to make contact are apparent on both sides. Marxists continued in the tradition of ignoring psychology; Freud and his disciples developed their ideas within the framework of mechanistic materialism, which proved restrictive to the development of the great discoveries of Freud and incompatible with "historical materialism."

In the meantime, new developments have occurred. The most important one is the revival of Marxist humanism. Many Marxist socialists in the smaller socialist countries especially, but also those in the West, have become aware of the fact that Marxist theory is in need of a psychological theory of man; they have also become aware of the fact that socialism must satisfy man's need for a system of orientation and devotion; that it must deal with the questions of who man is and what the meaning and aim of his life is. It must be the foundation for ethical norms and spiritual development beyond the empty phrases stating that "good is that which serves the revolution" (the worker's state, historical evolution, etc.).

On the other hand, the criticism arising in the psychoanalytic camp against the mechanistic materialism underlying Freud's thinking has led to a critical reevaluation of psychoanalysis, essentially of the libido theory. Because of the development in both Marxist and psychoanalytic thinking, the time seems to have come for humanist Marxists to recognize that the use of a dynamic, critical, socially oriented psychology is of crucial importance for the further development of Marxist theory and socialist practice; that a theory centered around man can no longer remain a theory without psychology if it is not to lose touch with human reality. In the following pages I want to point to some of the principal problems which have been dealt with or which ought to be treated by humanist psychoanalysis.[1]

The first problem which should be dealt with is that of the "social character," the character matrix common to a group (nation or class, for instance) which determines effectively the actions and thoughts of its members. This concept is a special development of Freud's character concept, the essence of which is the *dynamic* nature of character. Freud considered character as the relatively stable manifestation of various kinds of libidinous strivings, that is, of psychic energy directed to certain goals and stemming from certain sources. In his concepts of the oral, anal, and genital characters, Freud presented a new model of human character which explained behavior as the outcome of distinct passionate strivings; Freud assumed that the direction and intensity of these strivings was the result of early childhood experiences in relation to the "erogenous zones" (mouth, anus, genitals), and aside from constitutional elements the behavior of parents was mainly responsible for the libido development.

The concept of social character refers to the matrix of the character structure *common to a group*. It assumes that the fundamental factor in the formation of the social character is *the practice of life as it is constituted by the mode of production and the resulting social stratification*. The social character is *that particular structure of psychic energy which is molded by any given society so as to be useful for the functioning of that particular society*. The average person must *want* to do what he *has* to do in order to function in a way that permits society to use his energies for its purposes. Man's energy appears in the social process only partly as simple physical energy (laborers tilling the soil or building roads) and partly in *specific* forms of *psychic* energy. A member of a primitive people, living from assaulting and robbing other tribes, must have the character of a warrior, with a passion for war, killing, and robbing. The members of a peaceful, agricultural tribe must have an inclination for cooperation as against violence. Feudal society functions well only if its members have a striving for submission to authority, and respect and admiration for those who are their superiors. Capitalism functions only with men who are eager to work, who are disciplined and punctual, whose main interest is monetary gain, and whose main principle in life is profit as a result of production and exchange. In the nineteenth century capitalism needed men who liked to save; in the middle of the twentieth century it needs men who are passionately interested in spending and in consuming. The social character is the form in which human energy is molded for its use as a productive force in the social process.

The social character is reinforced by all the instruments of influence available to a society—its educational system, its religion, its literature, its songs, its jokes, its customs, and, most of all, its parents' methods of bringing up their children. This last is so important because the character structure of individuals is formed to a considerable extent in the first five or six years of their lives. But the influence of the parents is not essentially an individual or accidental one, as classic psychoanalysts believe. The parents are primarily the *agents of society*, both through their own characters and through their educational methods; they differ from each other only to a small degree, and these differences usually do not diminish their influence in creating the socially desirable matrix of the social character.

A condition for the formulation of the concept of the social character as being molded by the practice of life in any given society was a revision of Freud's libido theory, which is the basis for his concept of character. The libido theory is rooted in the mechanistic concept of man as a machine, with the libido (aside from the drive for self-preservation) as the energy source, governed by the "pleasure principle," the reduction of increased libidinal tension to its normal level. In contrast to this concept, I have tried to show (especially in *Man for Himself*) that the various strivings of man, who is primarily a social being, develop as a result of his need for "assimilation" (of things) and "socialization" (with people), and that the forms of assimilation and socialization that constitute his main passions depend on the social structure in which he exists. Man in this concept is seen as characterized by his passionate strivings toward objects—men and nature—and his need of relating himself to the world.

The concept of the social character answers important questions which were not dealt with adequately in Marxist theory.

Why is it that a society succeeds in gaining the allegiance of most of its members, even when they suffer under the system and even if their reason tells them that their allegiance to it is harmful to them? Why has their *real* interest as human beings not outweighed their *fictitious* interests produced by all kinds of ideological influences and brainwashing? Why has consciousness of their class situation and of the advantages of socialism not been as effective as Marx believed it would be? The answer to this question lies in the phenomenon of the social character. Once a society has succeeded in molding the character structure of the average person in such a way that he likes to do that which he has to do, he is satisfied with the very conditions that society imposes upon him. As one of Ibsen's characters once said, "He can do anything he wants to do because he wants only what he can do." Needless to say, a social character which is, for instance, satisfied with submission is a crippled character. But crippled or not, it serves the purpose of a society requiring submissive men for its proper functioning.

The concept of the social character also serves to explain the link between the material basis of a society and the "ideological superstructure." Marx has often been interpreted as implying that the ideological superstructure was nothing but the reflection of the economic basis. This interpretation is not correct; but the fact is that in Marx's theory the nature of the relation between basis and super-structure was not sufficiently explained. A dynamic psychological theory can show that society produces the social character, and that the social character tends to produce and to hold onto ideas and ideologies which fit it and are nourished by it. However, it is not only the economic basis which creates a certain social character which, in turn, creates certain ideas. The ideas, once created, also influence the social character and, indirectly, the social economic structure. What I emphasize here is that *the social character is the intermediary between the socioeconomic structure and the ideas and ideals prevalent in a society*. It is the intermediary in both directions, from the economic basis to the ideas and from the ideas to the economic basis. The following scheme expresses this concept:

ECONOMIC BASIS
↓ SOCIAL CHARACTER
↓ IDEAS AND IDEALS

The concept of social character can explain how human energy, like any other raw material, is used by a society for the needs and purposes of that society. Man, in fact, is one of the most pliable natural forces; he can be made to serve almost any purpose; he can be made to hate or to cooperate, to submit or to stand up, to enjoy suffering or happiness.

While all this is true, it is also true that man can solve the problem of his existence only by the full unfolding of his human powers. The more crippled a society makes man, the sicker he becomes, even though consciously he may be satisfied with his lot. But unconsciously he is dissatisfied; and this very dissatisfaction is the element which inclines him eventually to change the social forms that cripple him. If he cannot do this, his particular kind of pathogenic society will die out. Social change and revolution are caused not only by new productive forces which conflict with older forms of social organization, but also by the conflict between inhuman social conditions and unalterable human needs. One can do almost anything to man, yet only almost. The history of man's fight for freedom is the most telling manifestation of this principle.

The concept of social character is not only a theoretical one lending itself to general speculation; it is useful and important for empirical studies which aim at finding out what the incidence of various kinds of social character is in a given society or social class. Assuming that one defines the "peasant character" as individualistic, hoarding, stubborn, with little satisfaction in cooperation, little sense of time and punctuality, this syndrome of traits is by no means a summation of various traits, but a structure, charged with energy. This structure will show intensive resistance by either violence or silent obstructionism if attempts are made to change it; even economic advantages will not easily produce any effects. The syndrome owes its existence to the common mode of production which has been characteristic of peasant life for thousands of years. The same holds true for a declining lower–middle class, whether it is that which brought Hitler to power, or the poor whites in the South of the United States. The lack of any kind of positive cultural stimulation, the resentment against their situation, which is one of being left behind by the forward-moving currents of their society, the hate toward those who destroyed the images which once gave them pride, have created a character syndrome which is made up of love of death (necrophilia), intense and malignant fixation to blood and soil, and intense group narcissism (the latter expressed in intense nationalism and racism).[2] One last example: the character structure of the industrial worker contains punctuality, discipline, capacity for teamwork; this is the syndrome which forms the minimum for the efficient functioning of an industrial worker. (Other differences—dependence-independence, interest-indifference, activity-passivity—are at this point ignored, although they are of utmost importance for the character structure of the worker now and in the future.)

The most important application of the concept of the social character lies in distinguishing the future social character of a socialist society as visualized by Marx from the social character of nineteenth-century capitalism, with its central desire for possession of property and wealth; and distinguishing it from the social character of the twentieth century (capitalist or communist), which is becoming ever more prevalent in the highly industrialized societies—the character of *homo consumens*.

Homo consumens is the man whose main goal is not primarily to *own* things, but to *consume* more and more, and thus to compensate for his inner vacuity, passivity, loneliness, and anxiety. In a society characterized by giant enterprises and giant industrial, governmental and labor bureaucracies, the individual, who has no control over his circumstances of work, feels impotent, lonely, bored, and anxious. At the same time, the need for profit of the big consumer industries, through the medium of advertising, transforms him into a voracious man, an eternal suckling who wants to consume more and more and for whom everything becomes an article of consumption—cigarettes, liquor, sex, movies, television, travel, and even education, books, and lectures. New artificial needs are created and man's tastes are manipulated. (The character of *homo consumens* in its more extreme forms is a well-known psychopathological phenomenon. It is to be found in many cases of depressed or anxious persons who escape into overeating, overbuying, or alcoholism to compensate for the hidden depression and anxiety.) The greed for consumption, an extreme form of what Freud called the "oral-receptive character," is becoming the dominant psychic force in present-day industrialized society. *Homo consumens* is under the illusion of happiness, while unconsciously he suffers from his boredom and passivity. The more power he has over machines, the more powerless he becomes as a human being; the more he consumes, the more he becomes a slave to the ever-increasing needs which the industrial system creates and manipulates. He mistakes thrill and excitement for joy and happiness and material comfort for aliveness; satisfied greed becomes the meaning of life, the striving for it a new religion. The freedom to consume becomes the essence of human freedom.

This spirit of consumption is precisely the opposite of the spirit of a socialist society as Marx visualized it. He clearly saw the danger inherent in capitalism. His aim was a society in which man *is* much, not in which he *has* or *uses* much. He wanted to liberate man from the chains of his material greed so that he could become fully awake, alive, and sensitive, and not be the slave of his greed. "The production of too many useful things," Marx wrote, "results in the creation of too many useless people." He wanted to abolish extreme poverty, because it prevents man from becoming fully human; he also wanted to prevent extreme wealth, in which the individual becomes the prisoner of his greed. His aim was not the *maximum* but the *optimum* of consumption, the satisfaction of those genuine human needs which serve as a means to a fuller and richer life.

It is one of the historical ironies that the spirit of capitalism, the satisfaction of material greed, is conquering the communist and socialist countries which, with their planned economy, would have the means to curb it. This process has its own logic; the material success of capitalism was immensely impressive to those poorer countries in Europe in which communism had been victorious, and the victory of socialism became identified with successful competition with capitalism *within* the spirit of capitalism. Socialism is in danger of deteriorating into a system which can accomplish the industrialization of poorer countries more quickly than capitalism, rather than of becoming a society in which the development of man, and not that of economic production, is the main goal. This development has been furthered by the fact that Soviet communism, in accepting a crude version of Marx's "materialism," lost contact, as did the capitalist countries, with the humanist spiritual tradition of which Marx was one of the greatest representatives.

It is true that the socialist countries have still not solved the problem of satisfying the *legitimate* material needs of their populations (and even in the United States forty percent of the population is not "affluent"). But it is of the utmost importance that socialist economists, philosophers, and psychologists be aware of the danger that the goal of *optimal* consumption can easily change to that of *maximal* consumption. The task for the socialist theoreticians is to study the nature of human needs; to find criteria for the distinction between *genuine* human needs, the satisfaction of which makes man more alive and sensitive, and *synthetic* needs created by capitalism which tend to weaken man, to make him more passive and bored, a slave to his greed for things.

What I am stressing here is not that production as such should be restricted, but that, once the optimal needs of individual consumption are fulfilled, it should be channeled into more production of the means for social consumption such as schools, libraries, theaters, parks, hospitals, public transportation, etc. The ever-increasing individual consumption in the highly industrialized countries suggests that competition, greed, and envy are engendered not only by private property, but also by unlimited private consumption. Socialist theoreticians must not lose sight of the fact that the aim of a humanistic socialism is to build an industrial society whose mode of production shall serve the fullest development of the total man and not the creation of *homo consumens;* that socialist society is an industrial society fit for human beings to live in and to develop.

There are empirical methods which permit the study of the social character. The aim of such study is to discover the incidence of the various character syndromes within the population as a whole and within each class, the intensity of the various factors within the syndrome, and new or contradictory factors which have been caused by different socioeconomic conditions. All such variants permit an insight into the strength of the existing character structure, the process of change, and also what measures might facilitate such changes. Needless to say, such insight is important in countries in transition from agriculture to industrialism, as well as for the problem of the transition of the worker under capitalism or state capitalism, that is, under alienated conditions, to the conditions of authentic socialism. Furthermore, such studies are guides to political action. If I know only the political "opinions" of people as ascertained by the opinion polls, I know how they are likely to act in the immediate future. If I want to know the strength of psychic forces (which at the moment may not yet be manifest consciously) such as, for instance, racism, war- or peace-mindedness, such studies of character inform me of the strength and direction of the underlying forces which operate in the social process and which may become manifest only after some time.[3]

There is no space to discuss in detail the methods that can be used to obtain the character data mentioned above. What they all have in common is avoidance of the error of accepting ideologies (rationalizations) for expressions of the inner, and usually unconscious, reality. One method which has proved to be very useful is that of an open-ended questionnaire, the answers to which are interpreted as to their non-intended or unconscious meaning. Thus, when one answer to the question, "Who are the men in history whom you most admire?" is "Alexander the Great, Nero, Marx, and Lenin" and another answer is "Socrates, Pasteur, Marx, and Lenin," the inference is made that the first respondent is an admirer of power and strict authority, the second an admirer of those who work in the service of life and who are benefactors of mankind. By using an extended projective questionnaire it is possible to obtain a reliable picture of the character structure of a person.[4] Other projective tests—the analysis of favorite jokes, songs, stories, and observable behavior (especially the "small acts" so important for psychoanalytic observation)—help in obtaining correct results. Methodologically, the main emphasis in all these studies is on the mode of production and the resulting class stratification, on the most significant character traits and the syndromes they form, and on the relationship between these two sets of data. With the method of stratified samples, whole nations or large social classes can thus be studied by including less than a thousand persons in the investigation.

Another important aspect of analytic social psychology is what Freud called the "unconscious." But, while Freud was mainly concerned with individual repression, the student of Marxist social psychology will be most concerned with the "social unconscious." This concept refers to that repression of inner reality which is common to large groups. Every society must make every effort not to permit its members, or those of a particular class, to be aware of impulses which, if they were conscious, could lead to socially "dangerous" thoughts or actions. Effective censorship occurs, not at the level of the printed or spoken word, but by preventing thoughts from even becoming conscious, that is, by repression of dangerous awareness. Naturally the contents of the social unconscious vary depending on the many forms of social structure: aggressiveness, rebelliousness, dependency, loneliness, unhappiness, boredom, to mention only a few. The repressed impulse must be kept in repression and replaced by ideologies which deny it or affirm its opposite. The bored, anxious, unhappy man of today's industrial society is taught to think that he is happy and full of fun. In other societies the man deprived of freedom of thought and expression is taught to think that he has almost reached the most complete form of freedom, even though at the moment only his leaders speak in the name of that freedom. In some systems love of life is repressed and love of property is cultivated instead; in others, awareness of alienation is repressed, and instead the slogan, "there can be no alienation in a socialist country," is promoted.

Another way of expressing the phenomenon of the unconscious is to speak of it in the terms of Hegel and Marx, that is, as the totality of forces which work behind man's back while he has the illusion of being free in his decisions or, as Adam Smith put it, "economic man is led by an invisible hand to promote an end which was no part of his intention." While for Smith this invisible hand was a benevolent one, for Marx (as well as for Freud) it was a dangerous one; it had to be uncovered in order to be deprived of its effectiveness. Consciousness is a social phenomenon; for Marx it is mostly false consciousness, the work of the forces of repression.[5] The unconscious, like consciousness, is also a social phenomenon, determined by the "social filter" which does not permit most real human experiences to ascend from unconsciousness to consciousness. This social filter consists mainly of language, logic and social taboos; it is covered up by ideologies (rationalizations) which are subjectively experienced as being true, when in reality they are nothing but socially produced and shared fictions. This approach to consciousness and the repression can demonstrate empirically the validity of Marx's statement that "social existence determines consciousness."

As a consequence of these considerations, another theoretical difference between dogmatic Freudian- and Marxist-oriented psychoanalysis appears. Freud believed that the effective *cause for repression*—the most important content to be repressed being incestuous desires—is the fear of castration. I believe, on the contrary, that, individually and socially, man's greatest fear is that of complete isolation from his fellow men, of complete ostracism. Even fear of death is easier to bear. Society enforces its demands for repression by the threat of ostracism. If you do not deny the presence of certain experiences, you do not belong, you belong nowhere, you are in danger of becoming insane. (Insanity is, in fact, the illness characterized by total absence of relatedness to the world outside.)

Marxists have usually assumed that what works behind man's back and directs him are economic forces and their political representations. Psychoanalytic study shows that this is much too narrow a concept. Society consists of people, and each person is equipped with a potential of passionate strivings, from the most archaic to the most progressive. This human potential as a whole is molded by the ensemble of economic and social forces characteristic of each given society. These forces of the social ensemble produce a certain social unconscious, and certain conflicts between the repressive factors and given human needs which are essential for sane human functioning (like a certain degree of freedom, stimulation, interest in life, happiness). In fact, as I said before, revolutions occur as expressions of not only new productive forces, but also of the repressed part of human nature, and they are successful only when the two conditions are combined. Repression, whether it is individually or socially conditioned, distorts man, fragments him, deprives him of his whole humanity. Consciousness represents the "social man" determined by a given society; the unconscious represents the universal man in us, the good and the bad, the whole man who justifies Terence's saying, "I believe that nothing human is alien to me." (This incidentally was Marx's favorite motto.)

Depth psychology also has a contribution to make to a problem which plays a central role in Marx's theory, even though Marx never arrived at its satisfactory solution: the problem of the essence and nature of man. On the one hand Marx—especially after 1844—did not want to use a metaphysical, unhistorical concept like the "essence of man," a concept which had been used for thousands of years by many rulers in order to prove that their rules and laws corresponded to what each declared to be the unchangeable "nature of man." On the other hand, Marx was opposed to a relativistic view that man is born a blank piece of paper on which every culture writes its text. If this were true, how could man ever rebel against the forms of existence into which a given society forces its members? How could Marx use (in *Capital*) the concept of the "crippled man" if he did not have a concept of a "model of human nature" which *could* be crippled? An answer on the basis of psychological analysis lies in the assumption that there is no "essence of man," in the sense of a *substance* which remains the same throughout history. The answer, in my opinion, is to be found in the fact that man's essence lies in the very contradiction between his being *in* nature, thrown into the world without his will and taken away against his will, at an accidental place and time, and at the same time *transcending* nature by his lack of instinctual equipment and by the fact of his awareness—of himself, of others, of the past and the present. Man, a "freak of nature," would feel unbearably alone unless he could solve his contradiction by finding a new form of unity. The essential contradiction in man's existence forces him to seek a solution of this contradiction, to find an answer to the question which life asks him from the moment of his birth. There are a number of ascertainable but limited answers to the question of how to find unity. Man can find unity by trying to regress to the animal stage, by doing away with what is specifically human (reason and love), by being a slave or a slave driver, by transforming himself into a thing, or else by developing his specific human powers to such an extent that he finds a new unity with his fellow man and with nature by becoming a free man—free not only *from* chains but free *to* make the development of all his potentialities the very aim of his life—a man who owes his existence to his own productive effort. Man has no innate "drive for progress," but he is driven by the need to solve his existential contradiction, which arises again at every new level of development. This contradiction—or, in other words, man's different and contradictory possibilities—constitutes his essence.

To sum up: this article is a plea to introduce a dialectically and humanistically oriented psychoanalysis as a significant viewpoint into Marxist thought. *I believe that Marxism needs such a psychological theory and that psychoanalysis needs to incorporate genuine Marxist theory. Such a synthesis will fertilize both fields.*

Notes

1. Unfortunately there are so few authors who have attempted to apply revised psychoanalysis to the problem of Marxism and socialism that I must refer mainly to my own writings since 1930. Cf. especially *The Dogma of Christ* (New York: Rinehart and Winston, 1963); *Psychoanalytic Characterology and Its Relevance for Social Psychology*, in: *The Crisis of Psychoanalysis* (New York: Holt, Rinehart and Winston, 1970); *Escape from Freedom* (New York: Holt, Rinehart & Winston, 1941); *The Sane Society* (New York: Holt, Rinehart and Winston, 1955); *Marx's Concept of Man* (New York, Frederick Ungar & Co., 1961); *Beyond the Chains of Illusion* (New York: Pocket Books: Credo Series, ed. R. N. Anshen, 1962) deals explicitly with the relationship between the theories of Marx and Freud. Among other writers writing from a psychoanalytic-Marxist standpoint the most important is Wilhelm Reich, even though there is little in common between his theories and mine. Sartre's attempts at developing a Marxist-oriented humanist analysis suffers from the fact that he has little clinical experience and, on the whole, deals with psychology superficially even though in brilliant verbiage.

2. Cf. the detailed discussion of this point in E. Fromm, *The Heart of Man, Its Genius for Good and Evil* (New York: Harper and Row: Religious Perspectives Series, ed. R. N. Anshen, 1964).

3. Thus, for instance, the destructiveness present in the German lower middle class became manifest only when Hitler gave it the opportunity to express itself.

4. This method was first applied by myself together with Dr. E. Schachtel, Dr. P. Lazarsfeld, and others at the Institute of Social Research (Frankfurt University) in 1931 and later at Columbia University. The goal of the investigation was to find the incidence of authoritarian vs. anti-authoritarian characters among German workers and employees. The results corresponded pretty closely to the facts as shown by subsequent historical development. The same method has been employed in a psychosocial study of a small Mexican village, supported by the Foundations Fund for Research in Psychiatry, under my direction, with the assistance of Dr. Theodore and Dr. Lola Schwartz and Dr. Michael Maccoby. The statistical methods of Dr. Louis McQuitty make it possible to handle the hundreds of thousands of single data in such a way that, by using electronic computers, syndromes of typically related traits appear with all clarity. Cf. E. Fromm, *Deutsche Arbeiter und Angestellte am Vorabend des Dritten Reiches. Eine sozialpsychologische Untersuchung*, edited by W. Bonss (Stuttgart: Deutsche Verlags-Anstalt, 1980) and E. Fromm and M. Maccoby, *Social Character in a Mexican Village. A Sociopsychoanalytic Study* (Englewood Cliffs: Prentice Hall, 1970).

5. It is interesting to note that Marx used the term repression—"*Verdrängung*"—in the *German Ideology*. Rosa Luxemburg spoke of the unconscious (the logic of the historic process) coming before the conscious (the subjective logic of the human being) in *Leninism and Marxism*, recently published in English in *The Russian Revolution and Leninism or Marxism?* (Ann Arbor: University of Michigan Press, 1961).

IV.   Prophets and Priests

It can be said without exaggeration that never was the knowledge of the great ideas produced by the human race as widespread in the world as it is today, and never were these ideas less effective than they are today. The ideas of Plato and Aristotle, of the prophets and of Christ, of Spinoza and Kant, are known to millions among the educated classes in Europe and America. They are taught at thousands of institutions of higher learning, and some of them are preached in the churches of all denominations everywhere. And all this in a world which follows the principles of unrestricted egotism, which breeds hysterical nationalism, and which is preparing for an insane mass slaughter. How can one explain this discrepancy?

Ideas do not influence man deeply when they are only taught as ideas and thoughts. Usually, when presented in such a way, they change other ideas; new thoughts take the place of old thoughts; new words take the place of old words. But all that has happened is a change in concepts and words. Why should it be different? It is exceedingly difficult for a man to be moved by ideas, and to grasp a truth. In order to do that, he needs to overcome deep-seated resistances of inertia, fear of being wrong, or of straying away from the herd. Just to become acquainted with other ideas is not enough, even though these ideas in themselves are right and potent. But ideas do have an effect on man if the idea is lived by the one who teaches it; if it is personified by the teacher, if the idea appears in the flesh. If a man expresses the idea of humility and is humble, then those who listen to him will understand what humility is. They will not only understand, but they will believe that he is talking about a reality, and not just voicing words. The same holds true for all ideas which a man, a philosopher, or a religious teacher may try to convey.

Those who announce ideas—and not necessarily new ones—and at the same time live them we may call *prophets.* The Old Testament prophets did precisely that: they announced the idea that man had to find an answer to his existence, and that this answer was the development of his reason, of his love; and they taught that humility and justice were inseparably connected with love and reason. They lived what they preached. They did not seek power, but avoided it. Not even the power of being a prophet. They were not impressed by might, and they spoke the truth even if this led them to imprisonment, ostracism or death. They were not men who set themselves apart and waited to see what would happen. They responded to their fellow man because they felt responsible. What happened to others happened to them. Humanity was not outside, but within them. Precisely because they saw the truth they felt the responsibility to tell it; they did not threaten, but they showed the *alternatives* with which man was confronted. It is not that a prophet wishes to be a prophet; in fact, only the false ones have the ambition to become prophets. His becoming a prophet is simple enough, because the alternatives which he sees are simple enough. The prophet Amos expressed this idea very succinctly: "The lion has roared, who will not be afraid. God has spoken, who will not be a prophet." The phrase "God has spoken" here means simply that the choice has become unmistakably clear. There can be no more doubt. There can be no more evasion. Hence the man who feels responsible has no choice but to become a prophet, whether he has been herding sheep, tending his vineyards, or developing and teaching ideas. It is the function of the prophet to show reality, to show alternatives and to protest; it is his function to call loudly, to awake man from his customary half-slumber. It is the historical situation which makes prophets, not the wish of some men to be prophets.

Many nations have had their prophets. The Buddha lived his teachings; Christ appeared in the flesh; Socrates died according to his ideas; Spinoza lived them. And they all made a deep imprint on the human race precisely because their idea was manifested in the flesh in each one of them.

Prophets appear only at intervals in the history of humanity. They die and leave their message. The message is accepted by millions, it becomes dear to them. This is precisely the reason why the idea becomes exploitable for others who can make use of the attachment of the people to these ideas, for their own purposes—those of ruling and controlling. Let us call the men who make use of the idea the prophets have announced the *priests*. The prophets live their ideas. The priests administer them to the people who are attached to the idea. The idea has lost its vitality. It has become a formula. The priests declare that it is very important how the idea is formulated; naturally the formulation becomes always important after the experience is dead; how else could one control people by controlling their thoughts, unless there is the "correct" formulation? The priests use the idea to organize men, to control them through controlling the proper expression of the idea, and when they have anesthetized man enough they declare that man is not capable of being awake and of directing his own life, and that they, the priests, act out of duty, or even compassion, when they fulfill the function of directing men who, if left to themselves, are afraid of freedom. It is true not all priests have acted that way, but most of them have, especially those who wielded power.

There are priests not only in religion. There are priests in philosophy and priests in politics. Every philosophical school has its priests. Often they are very learned; it is their business to administer the idea of the original thinker, to impart it, to interpret it, to make it into a museum object and thus to guard it. Then there are the political priests; we have seen enough of them in the last 150 years. They have administered the idea of freedom, to protect the economic interests of their social class. In the twentieth century the priests have taken over the administration of the ideas of socialism. While this idea aimed at the liberation and independence of man, the priests declared in one way or another that man was not capable of being free, or at least that he would not be for a long time. Until then they were obliged to take over, and to decide how the idea was to be formulated, and who was a faithful believer and who was not. The priests usually confuse the people because they claim that they are the successors of the prophet, and that they live what they preach. Yet, while a child could see that they live precisely the opposite of what they teach, the great mass of the people are brainwashed effectively, and eventually they come to believe that if the priests live in splendor they do so as a sacrifice, because they have to represent the great idea; or if they kill ruthlessly they only do so out of revolutionary faith.

No historical situation could be more conducive to the emergence of prophets than ours. The existence of the entire human race is threatened by the madness of preparing nuclear war. Stone-age mentality and blindness have led to the point where the human race seems to be moving rapidly toward the tragic end of its history at the very moment when it is near to its greatest achievement. At this point humanity needs prophets, even though it is doubtful whether their voices will prevail against that of the priests.

Among the few in whom the idea has become manifest in

the flesh, and whom the historical situation of mankind has transformed from teachers into prophets, is Bertrand Russell. He happens to be a great thinker, but that is not really essential to his being a prophet. He, together with Einstein and Schweitzer, represents the answer of Western humanity to the threat to its existence, because all three of them have spoken up, have warned, and have pointed out the alternatives. Schweitzer lived the idea of Christianity by working in Lambaréné. Einstein lived the idea of reason and humanism by refusing to join the hysterical voices of nationalism of the German intelligentsia in 1914 and many times after that. Bertrand Russell for many decades expressed his ideas on rationality and humanism in his books; but in recent years he has gone out to the marketplace to show all men that when the laws of the country contradict the laws of humanity, a true man must choose the laws of humanity.

Bertrand Russell has recognized that the idea, even if embodied in one person, gains social significance only if it is embodied in a group. When Abraham argued with God about Sodom's fate, and challenged God's justice, he asked that Sodom be spared if there were only ten just men, but not less. If there were less than ten, that is to say, if there were not even the smallest group in which the idea of justice had become embodied, even Abraham could not expect the city to be saved. Bertrand Russell tries to prove that there are the ten who can save the city. That is why he has organized people, has marched with them, and has sat down with them and been carried off with them in police vans. While his voice is a voice in the wilderness it is, nevertheless, not an isolated voice. It is the leader of a chorus; whether it is the chorus of a Greek tragedy or that of Beethoven's Ninth Symphony only the history of the next few years will reveal.

Among the ideas which Bertrand Russell embodies in his life, perhaps the first one to be mentioned is man's right and duty to disobedience.

By disobedience I do not refer to the disobedience of the "rebel without cause" who disobeys because he has no commitment to life except the one to say "no." This kind of rebellious disobedience is as blind and impotent as its opposite, the conformist obedience which is *incapable* of saying "no." I am speaking of the man who can say "no" because he can affirm, who can disobey precisely because he can obey his conscience and the principles which he has chosen; I am speaking of the revolutionary, not the rebel.

In most social systems obedience is the supreme virtue, disobedience the supreme sin. In fact, in our culture when most people feel "guilty," they are actually feeling afraid because they have been disobedient. They are not really troubled by a moral issue, as they think they are, but by the fact of having disobeyed a command. This is not surprising; after all, Christian teaching has interpreted Adam's disobedience as a deed which corrupted him and his seed so fundamentally that only the special act of God's grace could save man from this corruption. This idea was, of course, in accord with the social function of the Church which supported the power of the rulers by teaching the sinfulness of disobedience. Only those men who took seriously the biblical teachings of humility, brotherliness, and justice rebelled against secular authority, with the result that the Church, more often than not, branded them as rebels and sinners against God. Mainstream Protestantism did not alter this. On the contrary, while the Catholic Church kept alive the awareness of the difference between secular and spiritual authority, Protestantism allied itself with secular power. Luther was only giving the first and drastic expression to this trend when he wrote about the revolutionary German peasants of the sixteenth century, "Therefore let us everyone who can, smite, slay and stab, secretly or openly, remembering that nothing can be more poisonous, hurtful or devilish than a rebel."

In spite of the vanishing of religious terror, authoritarian political systems continued to make obedience the human cornerstone of their existence. The great revolutions in the seventeenth and eighteenth centuries fought against royal authority, but soon man reverted to making a virtue of obedience to the king's successors, whatever name they took. Where is authority today? In the totalitarian countries it is overt authority of the state, supported by the strengthening of respect for authority in the family and in the school. The Western democracies, on the other hand, feel proud at having overcome nineteenth-century authoritarianism. But have they—or has only the character of the authority changed?

This century is the century of the hierarchically organized bureaucracies in government, business, and labor unions. These bureaucracies administer things *and* men as one; they follow certain principles, especially the economic principle of the balance sheet, quantification, maximal efficiency, and profit, and they function essentially as would an electronic computer that has been programmed with these principles. The individual becomes a number, transforms himself into a thing. But just because there is no overt authority, because he is not "forced" to obey, the individual is under the illusion that he acts voluntarily, that he follows only "rational" authority. Who can disobey the "reasonable"? Who can disobey the computer-bureaucracy? Who can disobey when he is not even aware of obeying? In the family and in education the same thing happens. The corruption of the theories of progressive education have led to a method where the child is not told what to do, not given orders, nor punished for failure to execute them. The child just "expresses himself." But, from the first day of his life onward, he is filled with an unholy respect for conformity, with the fear of being "different," with the fright of being away from the rest of the herd. The "organization man" thus reared in the family and in the school and having his education completed in the big organization has opinions, but no convictions; he amuses himself, but is unhappy; he is even willing to sacrifice his life and that of his children in voluntary obedience to impersonal and anonymous powers. He accepts the calculation of deaths which has become so fashionable in the discussions on thermonuclear war: half the population of a country dead—"quite acceptable"; two-thirds dead—"maybe not."

The question of disobedience is of vital importance today. While, according to the Bible, human history began with an act of disobedience—Adam and Eve—while, according to Greek myth, civilization began with Prometheus' act of disobedience, it is not unlikely that human history will be terminated by an act of obedience, by the obedience to authorities who themselves are obedient to archaic fetishes of "State sovereignty," "national honor," "military victory," and who will give the orders to push the fatal buttons to those who are obedient to them and to their fetishes.

Disobedience, then, in the sense in which we use it here, is an act of the affirmation of reason and will. It is not primarily an attitude directed *against* something, but *for* something: for man's capacity to see, to say what he sees, and to refuse to say what he does not see. To do so he does not need to be aggressive or rebellious; he needs to have his eyes open, to be fully awake, and willing to take the responsibility to open the eyes of those who are in danger of perishing because they are half asleep.

Karl Marx once wrote that Prometheus, who said that he "would rather be chained to his rock than to be the obedient servant of the gods," is the patron saint of all philosophers. This consists in renewing the Promethean function of life itself. Marx's statement points very clearly to the problem of the connection between philosophy and disobedience. Most philosophers were not disobedient to the authorities of their time. Socrates obeyed by dying, Spinoza declined the position of a professor rather than to find himself in conflict with authority, Kant was a loyal citizen, Hegel exchanged his youthful revolutionary sympathies for the glorification of the State in his later years. Yet, in spite of this, Prometheus was their patron saint. It is true, they remained in their lecture halls and their studies and did not go to the marketplace, and there were many reasons for this which I shall not discuss now. But as philosophers they were disobedient to the authority of traditional thoughts and concepts, to the clichés which were believed and taught. They were bringing light to darkness, they were waking up those who were half asleep, they "dared to know."

The philosopher is disobedient to clichés and to public opinion because he is obedient to reason and to mankind. It is precisely because reason is universal and transcends all national borders, that the philosopher who follows reason is a citizen of the world; man is his object—not this or that person, this or that nation. The world is his country, not the place where he was born.

Nobody has expressed the revolutionary nature of thought more brilliantly than Bertrand Russell. In *Principles of Social Reconstruction* (1916), he wrote:

Men fear thought more than they fear anything else on earth—more than ruin, more even than death. Thought is subversive and revolutionary, destructive and terrible; thought is merciless to privilege, established institutions, and comfortable habits; thought is anarchic and lawless, indifferent to authority, careless of the well-tried wisdom of the ages. Thought looks into the pit of hell and is not afraid. It sees man, a feeble speck, surrounded by unfathomable depths of silence; yet bears itself proudly, as unmoved as if it were lord of the universe. Thought is great and swift and free, the light of the world, and the chief glory of man.

But if thought is to become the possession of many, not the privilege of the few, we must have done with fear. It is fear that holds men back—fear lest their cherished beliefs should prove delusions, fear lest the institutions by which they live should prove harmful, fear lest they themselves should prove less worthy of respect than they have supposed themselves to be. "Should the working man think freely about property? Then what will become of us, the rich? Should young men and young women think freely about sex? Then what will become of morality? Should soldiers think freely about war? Then what will become of military discipline? Away with thought! Back into the shades of prejudice, lest property, morals, and war should be endangered! Better men should be stupid, slothful, and oppressive than that their thoughts should be free. For if their thoughts were free they might not think as we do. And at all costs this disaster must be averted." So the opponents of thought argue in the unconscious depths of their souls. And so they act in their churches, their schools, and their universities.

Bertrand Russell's capacity to disobey is rooted, not in some abstract principle, but in the most real experience there is—in the love of life. This love of life shines through his writings as well as through the person. It is a rare quality today, and especially rare in the very countries where men live in the midst of plenty. Many confuse thrill with joy, excitement with interest, consuming with being. The necrophilous slogan "Long live death," while consciously used only by the fascists, fills the hearts of many people living in the lands of plenty, although they are not aware of it themselves. It seems that in this fact lies one of the reasons which explain why the majority of people are resigned to accept nuclear war and the ensuing destruction of civilization and take so few steps to prevent this catastrophe. Bertrand Russell, on the contrary, fights against the threatening slaughter, not because he is a pacifist or because some abstract principle is involved, but precisely because he is a man who loves life.

For the very same reason he has no use for those voices which love to harp on the evilness of man, in fact thus saying more about themselves and their own gloomy moods than about men. Not that Bertrand Russell is a sentimental romantic. He is a hard-headed, critical, caustic realist; he is aware of the depth of evil and stupidity to be found in the heart of man, but he does not confuse this fact with an alleged innate corruption which serves to rationalize the outlook of those who are too gloomy to believe in man's gift to create a world in which he can feel himself to be at home. "Except for those rare spirits," wrote Russell in *Mysticism and Logic: A Free Man's Worship* (1903), "that are born without sin, there is a cavern of darkness to be traversed before that temple can be entered. The gate of the cavern is despair, and its floor is paved with the gravestones of abandoned hopes. There Self must die; there the eagerness, the greed of untamed desire must be slain, for only so can the soul be freed from the empire of Fate. But out of the cavern the Gate of Renunciation leads again to the daylight of wisdom, by whose radiance a new insight, a new joy, a new tenderness, shine forth to gladden the pilgrim's heart." And later, in *Philosophical Essays* (1910), he wrote: "But for those who feel that life on this planet would be a life in prison if it were not for the windows onto a greater world beyond; for those to whom a belief in man's omnipotence seems arrogant, who desire rather the Stoic freedom that comes of mastery over the passions than the Napoleonic domination that sees the kingdoms of this world at its feet—in a word, to men who do not find Man an adequate object of their worship, the pragmatist's world will seem narrow and petty, robbing life of all that gives it value, and making Man himself smaller by depriving the universe which he contemplates of all its splendour." His views on the alleged evilness of man, Russell expressed brilliantly in the *Unpopular Essays* (1950): "Children, after being limbs of Satan in traditional theology and mystically illuminated angels in the minds of educational reformers, have reverted to being little devils—not theological demons inspired by the Evil One, but scientific Freudian abominations inspired by the Unconscious. They are, it must be said, far more wicked than they were in the diatribes of the monks; they display, in modern textbooks, an ingenuity and persistence in sinful imaginings to which in the past there was nothing comparable except St. Anthony. Is all this the objective truth at last? Or is it merely an adult imaginative compensation for being no longer allowed to wallop the little pests? Let the Freudians answer, each for the others." One more quotation from Russell's writings which shows how deeply this humanist thinker has experienced this joy of living. "The lover," he wrote in *The Scientific Outlook* (1931), "the poet, and the mystic find a fuller satisfaction than the seeker after power can ever know, since they can retain the object of their love, whereas the seeker after power must be perpetually engaged in some fresh manipulation if he is not to suffer from a sense of emptiness. When I come to die I shall not feel I have lived in vain. I have seen the earth turn red at evening, the dew sparkling in the morning, and the snow shining under a frosty sun; I have smelt rain after drought, and have heard the stormy Atlantic beat upon the granite shores of Cornwall. Science may bestow these and other joys among more people than could otherwise enjoy them. If so, its power will be wisely used. But when it takes out of life the moments to which life owes its values, science will not deserve admiration, however cleverly and however elaborately it may lead men along the road to despair."

Bertrand Russell is a scholar, a man who believes in reason. But how different he is from the many men whose profession is the same: scholarship. With these the thing that counts is the intellectual grasp of the world. They feel certain that their intellect exhausts reality, and that there is nothing of significance which cannot be grasped by it. They are skeptical toward everything which cannot be caught in an intellectual formula, but they are naively unskeptical toward their own scientific approach. They are more interested in the results of their thoughts than in the process of enlightenment which occurs in the inquiring person.

Russell spoke of this kind of intellectual procedure when discussing pragmatism in his *Philosophical Essays* (1910): "Pragmatism," he wrote, "appeals to the temper of mind which finds on the surface of this planet the whole of its imaginative material; which feels confident of progress, and unaware of nonhuman limitations to human power; which loves battle, with all the attendant risks, because it has no real doubt that it will achieve victory; which desires religion, as it desires railways and electric light, as a comfort and a help in the affairs of this world, not as providing nonhuman objects to satisfy the hunger for perfection and for something to be worshipped without reserve."

For Russell, in contrast to the pragmatist, rational thought is not the quest for certainty, but an adventure, an act of self-liberation and of courage, which changes the thinker by making him more awake and more alive.

Bertrand Russell is a man of faith. Not of faith in the theological sense, but of faith in the power of reason, faith in man's capacity to create his own paradise through his own efforts. "As geological time is reckoned," so he wrote in *Man's Peril from the Hydrogen Bomb* (1954), "Man has so far existed only for a very short period—1,000,000 years at the most. What he has achieved, especially during the last 6,000 years, is something utterly new in the history of the Cosmos, so far at least as we are acquainted with it. For countless ages the sun rose and set, the moon waxed and waned, the stars shone in the night, but it was only with the coming of Man that these things were understood. In the great world of astronomy and in the little world of the atom, Man has unveiled secrets which might have been thought undiscoverable. In art and literature and religion, some men have shown a sublimity of feeling which makes the species worth preserving. Is all this to end in trivial horror because so few are able to think of Man rather than of this or that group of men? Is our race so destitute of wisdom, so incapable of impartial love, so blind even to the simplest dictates of self-preservation, that the last proof of its silly cleverness is to be the extermination of all life on our planet?—for it will be not only men who will perish, but also the animals and plants, whom no one can accuse of communism or anticommunism.

"I cannot believe that this is to be the end. I would have men forget their quarrels for a moment and reflect that, if they will allow themselves to survive, there is every reason to expect the triumphs of the future to exceed immeasurably the triumphs of the past. There lies before us, if we choose, continual progress in happiness, knowledge, and wisdom. Shall we, instead, choose death, because we cannot forget our quarrels? I appeal, as a human being to human beings: remember your humanity, and forget the rest. If you can do so, the way lies open to a new Paradise; if you cannot, nothing lies before you but universal death."

This faith is rooted in a quality without which neither his philosophy nor his fight against war could be understood: *his love for life.*

To many people this may not mean much; they believe that everybody loves life. Does he not cling to it when it is threatened, does he not have a great deal of fun in life and plenty of thrilling excitement?

In the first place, people do not cling to life when it is threatened; how else could one explain their passivity before the threat of nuclear slaughter? Furthermore, people confuse excitement with joy, thrill with love of life. They are "without joy in the midst of plenty." The fact is that all the virtues for which capitalism is praised—individual initiative, the readiness to take risks, independence—have long disappeared from industrial society and are to be found mainly in westerns and among gangsters. In bureaucratized, centralized industrialism, regardless of political ideology, there is an increasing number of people who are fed up with life and willing to die in order to get over their boredom. They are the ones who say "better dead than red," but deep down their motto is "better dead than alive." As I mentioned earlier, the extreme form of such an orientation was to be found among those fascists whose motto was "Long live death." Nobody recognized this more clearly than did Miguel de Unamuno when he spoke for the last time in his life at the University of Salamanca, where he was Rector at the time of the beginning of the Spanish Civil War; the occasion was a speech by General Millán Astray, whose favorite motto was "Viva la Muerte!" (Long live death!) and one of his followers shouted it from the back of the hall. When the general had finished his speech Unamuno rose and said: ". . . Just now I heard a necrophilous and senseless cry: 'Long live death!' And I, who have spent my life shaping paradoxes which have aroused the uncomprehending anger of others, I must tell you, as an expert authority, that this outlandish paradox is repellent to me. General Millán Astray is a cripple. Let is be said without any slighting undertone. He is a war invalid. So was Cervantes. Unfortunately there are too many cripples in Spain just now. And soon there will be even more of them if God does not come to our aid. It pains me to think that General Millán Astray should dictate the pattern of mass psychology. A cripple who lacks the spiritual greatness of a Cervantes is wont to seek ominous relief in causing mutilation around him." At this Millán Astray was unable to restrain himself any longer. *"Abajo la inteligencia!"* (Down with intelligence!) he shouted. "Long live death!" There was a clamor of support for this remark from the Falangists. But Unamuno went on: "This is the temple of the intellect. And I am its high priest. It is you who profane its sacred precincts. You will win, because you have more than enough brute force. But you will not convince. For to convince you need to persuade. And in order to persuade you would need what you lack: Reason and Right in the struggle. I consider it futile to exhort you to think of Spain. I have done."

However, the attraction to death which Unamuno called necrophilia is not a product of fascist thought alone. It is a phenomenon deeply rooted in a culture which is increasingly dominated by the bureaucratic organizations of the big corporations, governments, and armies, and by the central role of man-made things, gadgets, and machines. This bureaucratic industrialism tends to transform human beings into things. It tends to replace nature by technical devices, the organic by the inorganic.

One of the earliest expressions of this love for destruction and for machines, and of the contempt for woman (woman is a manifestation of life for man just as man is a manifestation of life for woman), is to be found in the futuristic manifesto (by Marinetti in 1909) one of the intellectual forerunners of Italian fascism. He wrote:

> . . . 4. We declare that the world's splendor has been enriched by a new beauty; the beauty of speed. A racing motor-car, its frame adorned with great pipes, like snakes with explosive breath . . . a roaring motor-car, which looks as though running on a shrapnel is more beautiful than the Victory of Samothrace.
>
> 5. We shall sing of the man at the steering wheel, whose ideal stem transfixes the Earth, rushing over the circuit of her orbit.
>
> . . . 8. Why should we look behind us, when we have to break in the mysterious portals of the Impossible? Time and Space died yesterday. Already we live in the absolute, since we have already created speed, eternal and ever-present.
>
> 9. We wish to glorify War—the only health-giver of the world—militarism, patriotism, the destructive arm of the Anarchist, the beautiful Ideas that kill, the contempt for woman.
>
> 10. We wish to destroy the museums, the libraries, to fight against moralism, feminism, and all opportunistic and utilitarian meannesses.

There is indeed no greater distinction among human beings than that between those who love life and those who love death. This love of death is a typically human acquisition. Man is the only animal that can be bored, he is the only animal that can love death. While the impotent man (I am not referring to sexual impotence) cannot create life, he can destroy it and thus transcend it. The love of death in the midst of living is the ultimate perversion. There are some who are the true necrophiles—and they salute war and promote it, even though they are mostly not aware of their motivation and rationalize their desires as serving life, honor, or freedom. They are probably the minority; but there are many who have never made the choice between life and death, and who have escaped in busy-ness in order to hide this. They do not salute destruction, but they also do not salute life. They lack the joy of life which would be necessary to oppose war vigorously.

Goethe once said that the most profound distinction between various historical periods is that between belief and disbelief, and added that all epochs in which belief dominates are brilliant, uplifting, and fruitful, while those in which disbelief dominates vanish because nobody cares to devote himself to the unfruitful. The "belief" Goethe spoke of is deeply rooted in the love of life. Cultures which create the conditions for loving life are also cultures of belief; those which cannot create this love also cannot create belief.

Bertrand Russell is a man of belief. In reading his books and in watching his activities for peace his love of life seems to me the mainspring of his whole person. He warns the world of impending doom precisely as the prophets did, because he loves life and all its forms and manifestations. He, again like the prophets, is not a determinist who claims that the historical future is already determined; he is an "alternativist" who sees that what is determined are certain limited and ascertainable alternatives. Our alternative is that between the end of the nuclear arms race—and destruction. Whether the voice of this prophet will win over the voices of doom and weariness depends on the degree of vitality the world and especially the younger generation has preserved. If we are to perish we cannot claim not to have been warned.

V. Let Man Prevail

When the medieval world was torn wide open, Western man seemed to be headed for the final fulfillment of his keenest dreams and visions. He freed himself from the authority of a totalitarian Church, the weight of traditional thought, the geographical limitations of a half-discovered globe. He discovered nature and the individual. He became aware of his own strength, of his capacity to make himself the ruler over nature and over traditionally given circumstances. He believed that he would be capable of achieving a synthesis between his newborn sense of strength and rationality and the spiritual values of his humanistic-spiritual tradition, between the prophetic idea of the messianic time of peace and justice to be achieved by mankind in the historical process and the Greek tradition of theoretical thought. In the centuries following the Renaissance and the Reformation, he built a new science which eventually led to the release of hitherto unheard-of productive powers and to the complete transformation of the material world. He created political systems which seem to guarantee the free and productive development of the individual; he reduced the time of work to such an extent that Western man is free to enjoy hours of leisure to an extent his forefathers had hardly dreamed of.

Yet where are we today?

The world is divided into two camps, the capitalist and the communist camp. Both camps believe that they have the key to the fulfillment of the human hopes of generations past; both maintain that, while they must coexist, their systems are incompatible.

Are they right? Are they not both in the process of converging into a new industrial neo-feudalism, into industrial societies, led and manipulated by big, powerful bureaucracies—societies in which the individual becomes a well-fed and well-entertained automaton who loses his individuality, his independence and his humanity? Have we to resign ourselves to the fact that we can master nature and produce goods in an ever-increasing degree, but that we must give up the hope for a new world of solidarity and justice; that this ideal will be lost in an empty technological concept of "progress"?

Is there no other alternative than that between capitalist and communist managerial industrialism? Can we not build an industrial society in which the individual retains his role as an active, responsible member who controls circumstances, rather than being controlled by them? Are economic wealth and human fulfillment really incompatible?

These two camps not only compete economically and politically, they are both set against each other in deadly fear of an atomic attack which will wipe out both, if not all civilization. Indeed, man has created the atomic bomb; it is the result of one of his greatest intellectual achievements. But he has lost the mastery over his own creation. The bomb has become his master, the forces of his own creation have become his most dangerous enemy.

Is there still time to reverse this course? Can we succeed in changing it and becoming the masters of circumstances, rather than allowing circumstances to rule us? Can we overcome the deep-seated roots of barbarism which make us try to solve problems in the only way in which they can *never* be solved—by force, violence, and killing? Can we close the gap between our great intellectual achievement and our emotional and moral backwardness?

In order to answer these questions, a more detailed examination of Western man's present position is necessary.

To most Americans the case for the success of our mode of industrial organization seems to be clear and overwhelming. New productive forces—steam, electricity, oil, and atomic energy—and new forms of organization of work—central planning, bureaucratization, increased division of labor, automation—have created a material wealth in the most advanced industrial countries which has done away with the extreme poverty in which the majority of their populations lived a hundred years ago.

Working hours have been reduced from seventy to forty hours per week in the last hundred years, and with increasing automation an ever-shorter working day may give man an undreamed-of amount of leisure. Basic education has been brought to every child; higher education to a considerable percentage of the total population. Movies, radio, television, sports, and hobbies fill out the many hours which man now has for his leisure.

Indeed, it seems that for the first time in history the vast majority—and soon all men—in the Western world will be primarily concerned with living, rather than with the struggle to secure the material conditions for living. It seems that the fondest dreams of our forefathers are close to their realization, and that the Western world has found the answer to the question what the "good life" is.

While the majority of men in North America and western Europe still share this outlook, there are an increasing number of thoughtful and sensitive persons who see the flaws in this enticing picture. They notice, first of all, that even within the richest country in the world, the U.S.A., about one-fifth of the population does not share in the good life of the majority, that a considerable number of our fellow citizens have not reached the material standard of living which is the basis for a dignified human existence. They are aware, furthermore, that more than two-thirds of the human race, those who for centuries were the object of Western colonialism, have a standard of living from ten to twenty times lower than ours, and have a life expectancy half that of the average American.

They are struck by the irrational contradictions which beset our system. While there are millions in our own midst, and hundreds of millions abroad, who do not have enough to eat, we restrict agricultural production and, in addition, spend hundreds of millions each year in storing our surplus. We have affluence, but we do not have amenity. We are wealthier, but we have less freedom. We consume more, but we are emptier. We have more atomic weapons, but we are more defenseless. We have more education, but we have less critical judgment and convictions. We have more religion, but we become more materialistic. We speak of the American tradition which, in fact, is the spiritual tradition of radical humanism, and we call "un-American" those who want to apply the tradition to present-day society.

However, even if we comfort ourselves, as many do, with the assumption that it is only a matter of a few generations until the West and eventually the whole world will have reached economic affluence, the question arises: *What has become of man and where is he going if we continue on the road our industrial system has taken?*

In order to understand how those elements by which our system succeeded in solving some of its *economic* problems are leading to an increasing failure to solve the *human* problem, it is necessary to examine the features which are characteristic of twentieth-century capitalism.

Concentration of capital led to the formation of giant enterprises, managed by hierarchically organized bureaucracies. Large agglomerations of workers work together, part of a vast organized production machine which, in order to run at all, must run smoothly, without friction, without interruption. The individual worker and clerk become a cog in this machine; their function and activities are determined by the whole structure of the organization in which they work. In the large enterprises, legal ownership of the means of production has become separated from the management and has lost importance. The big enterprises are run by bureaucratic management, which does not own the enterprise legally, but socially. These managers do not have the qualities of the old owner—individual initiative, daring, risk-taking—but the qualities of the bureaucrat—lack of individuality, impersonality, caution, lack of imagination. They administer things and persons, and relate to persons as to things. This managerial class, while it does not own the enterprise legally, controls it factually; it is responsible, in an effective way, neither to the stockholders nor to those who work in the enterprise. In fact, while the most important fields of production are in the hands of the large corporations, these corporations are practically ruled by their top employees. The giant corporations which control the economic, and to a large degree the political, destiny of the country constitute the very opposite of the democratic process; *they represent power without control by those submitted to it.*

Aside from the industrial bureaucracy, the vast majority of the population is administered by still other bureaucracies. First of all, by the governmental bureaucracy (including that of the armed forces) which influences and directs the lives of many millions in one form or another. More and more the industrial, military and governmental bureaucracies are becoming intertwined, both in their activities and, increasingly, in their personnel. With the development of ever greater enterprises, unions have also developed into big bureaucratic machines in which the individual member has very little to say. Many union chiefs are managerial bureaucrats, just as industrial chiefs are.

All these bureaucracies have no plan, and no vision; and due to the very nature of bureaucratic administration, this has to be so. When man is transformed into a thing and managed like a thing, his managers themselves become things; and things have no will, no vision, no plan.

With the bureaucratic management of people, the democratic process becomes transformed into a ritual. Whether it is a stockholders' meeting of a big enterprise, a political election or a union meeting, the individual has lost almost all influence to determine decisions and to participate actively in the making of decisions. Especially in the political sphere, elections become more and more reduced to plebiscites in which the individual can express preference for one of two slates of professional politicians, and the best that can be said is that he is governed with his consent. But the means to bring about this consent are those of suggestion and manipulation and, with all that, the most fundamental decisions—those of foreign policy which involve peace and war—are made by small groups which the average citizen hardly even knows.

The political ideas of democracy, as the founding fathers of the United States conceived them, were not purely political ideas. They were rooted in the spiritual tradition which came to us from prophetic Messianism, the gospels, humanism, and from the enlightenment philosophers of the eighteenth century. All these ideas and movements were centered around one hope: that man, in the course of his history, can liberate himself from poverty, ignorance and injustice, and that he can build a society of harmony, peace and union between man and man and between man and nature. The idea that history has a goal and the faith in man's perfectability within the historical process have been the most specific elements of Occidental thought. They are the soil in which the American tradition is rooted and from which it draws its strength and vitality. What has happened to the idea of the perfectability of man and of society? It has deteriorated into a flat concept of "progress," into a vision of the production of more and better *things,* rather than standing for the birth of the fully alive and productive *man.* Our political concepts have today lost their spiritual roots. They have become matters of expediency, judged by the criterion of whether they help us to a higher standard of living and to a more effective form of political administration. Having lost their roots in the hearts and longings of man, they have become empty shells, to be thrown away if expediency warrants it.

The individual is managed and manipulated not only in the sphere of production, but also in the sphere of consumption, which allegedly is the one in which the individual expresses his free choice. Whether it is the consumption of food, clothing, liquor, cigarettes, movies, or television programs, a powerful suggestion apparatus is employed with two purposes: first, to constantly increase the individual's appetite for new commodities, and second, to direct these appetites into the channels most profitable for industry. The very size of the capital investment in the consumer-goods industry and the competition between a few giant enterprises make it necessary not to leave consumption to chance, nor to leave the consumer a free choice of whether he wants to buy more and what he wants to buy. His appetites have to be constantly whetted, tastes have to be manipulated, managed, and made predictable. Man is transformed into the "consumer," the eternal suckling, whose one wish is to consume more and "better" things.

While our economic system has enriched man materially, it has impoverished him humanly. Notwithstanding all propaganda and slogans about the Western world's faith in God, its idealism, its spiritual concern, our system has created a materialistic culture and a materialistic man. During his working hours, the individual is managed as part of a production team. During his hours of leisure time, he is managed and manipulated to be the perfect consumer who likes what he is told to like and yet has the illusion that he follows his own tastes. All the time he is hammered at by

slogans, by suggestions, by voices of unreality which de-
prive him of the last bit of realism he may still have. From
childhood on, true convictions are discouraged. There is
little critical thought, there is little real feeling, and hence
only conformity with the rest can save the individual from
an unbearable feeling of loneliness and lostness. The individual does not experience himself as the active bearer of
his own powers and inner richness, but as an impoverished
"thing," dependent on powers outside of himself into
which he has projected his living substance. Man is alienated from himself and bows down before the works of his
own hands. He bows down before the things he produces,
before the State and before the leaders of his own making.
His own act becomes to him an alien power, standing over
and against him instead of being ruled by him. More than
ever in history the consolidation of our own product to an
objective force above us, outgrowing our control, defeating
our expectations, annihilating our calculations, is one of the
main factors determining our development. His products,
his machines, and the State have become the idols of modern man, and these idols represent his own life forces in
alienated form.

Indeed, Marx was right in recognizing that "the place of
all physical and mental senses has been taken by the self-
alienation of all these senses, by the sense of having. Private property has made us so stupid and impotent that
things become ours only if we *have* them, that is, if they
exist for us as capital, and are owned by us, eaten by us,
drunk by us; that is, used by us. We are poor in spite of all
our wealth because we *have* much, but we *are* little."

As a result, the average man feels insecure, lonely, depressed, and suffers from a lack of joy in the midst of
plenty. Life does not make sense to him; he is dimly aware
that the meaning of life cannot lie in being nothing but a
"consumer." He could not stand the joylessness and mean-
inglessness of life were it not for the fact that the system
offers him innumerable avenues of escape, ranging from

television to tranquilizers, which permit him to forget that he is losing more and more of all that is valuable in life. In spite of all slogans to the contrary, we are quickly approaching a society governed by bureaucrats who administer a mass-man, well fed, well taken care of, dehumanized and depressed. We produce machines that are like men and men who are like machines. That which was the greatest criticism of socialism fifty years ago—that it would lead to uniformity, bureaucratization, centralization, and a soulless materialism—is a reality of today's capitalism. We talk of freedom and democracy, yet an increasing number of people are afraid of the responsibility of freedom, and prefer the slavery of the well-fed robot; they have no faith in democracy and are happy to leave it to the political experts to make the decisions.

We have created a widespread system of communication by means of radio, television and newspapers. Yet people are misinformed and indoctrinated rather than informed about political and social reality. In fact, there is a degree of uniformity in our opinions and ideas which could be explained without difficulty if it were the result of political pressure and caused by fear. The fact is that all agree "voluntarily," in spite of the fact that our system rests exactly on the idea of the right to disagreement and on the predilection for diversity of ideas.

Doubletalk has become the rule in the free-enterprise countries, as well as among their opponents. The latter call dictatorship "people's democracies," the former call dictatorships "freedom-loving people" if they are political allies. Of the possibility of fifty million Americans being killed in an atomic attack, one speaks of the "hazards of war," and one talks of victory in a "showdown," when sane thinking makes it clear that there can be no victory for anyone in an atomic holocaust.

Education, from primary to higher education, has reached a peak. Yet, while people get more education, they have less reason, judgment, and conviction. At best their intelligence is improved, but their reason—that is, their capacity to penetrate through the surface and to understand the underlying forces in individual and social life—is impoverished more and more. Thinking is increasingly split from feeling, and the very fact that people tolerate the threat of an atomic war hovering over all mankind, shows that modern man has come to a point where his sanity must be questioned.

Man, instead of being the master of the machines he has built, has become their servant. But man is not made to be a thing, and with all the satisfactions of consumption, the life forces in man cannot be held in abeyance continuously. We have only one choice, and that is mastering the machine again, making production into a means and not an end, using it for the unfolding of man—or else the suppressed life energies will manifest themselves in chaotic and destructive forms. Man will want to destroy life rather than die of boredom.

Can we make our mode of social and economic organization responsible for this state of man? As was indicated above, our industrial system, its way of production and consumption, the relations between human beings which it fosters, creates precisely the human situation which has been described. Not because it *wants* to create it, not due to evil intentions of individuals, but because of the fact that the average man's character is formed by the practice of life which is provided by the structure of society.

No doubt the form which capitalism has taken in the twentieth century is very different from what it was in the nineteenth century—so different, in fact, that it is doubtful whether even the same term should be applied to both systems. The enormous concentration of capital in giant enterprises, the increasing separation of management from ownership, the existence of powerful trade unions, state subsidies for agriculture and for some parts of industry, the elements of the "welfare state," elements of price control and a directed market, and many more features radically distinguish twentieth-century capitalism from that of the past. Yet whatever terminology we choose, certain basic elements are common to the old and the new capitalism: the principle that not solidarity and love, but individualistic, egotistical action brings the best results for everybody; the belief that an impersonal mechanism, the market, should regulate the life of society, not the will, vision and planning of the people. Capitalism puts things (capital) higher than life (labor). Power follows from possession, not from activity. Contemporary capitalism creates additional obstacles for the unfolding of man. It needs smoothly working teams of workers, clerks, engineers, consumers; it needs them because big enterprises, led by bureaucracies, require this kind of organization and the "organization man" who fits into it. Our system must create people who fit its needs; it must create people who cooperate smoothly and in large numbers; people who want to consume more and more; people whose tastes are standardized and can be easily anticipated and influenced. It needs people who feel free and independent, not subject to any authority or principle of conscience, yet who are willing to be commanded to do what is expected of them, to fit into the social machine without friction; it needs people who can be guided without force, led without leaders, prompted without aim—except the aim to make good, to be on the move, to go ahead. Production is guided by the principle that capital investment must bring profit, rather than by the principle that the real needs of people determine what is to be produced. Since everything, including radio, television, books and medicines, is subject to the profit principle, the people are manipulated into the kind of consumption which is often poisonous for the spirit, and sometimes also for the body.

The failure of our society to fulfill the human aspirations rooted in our spiritual traditions has immediate consequences for the two most burning practical issues of our time: that of peace and that of the equalization between the wealth of the West and the poverty of two-thirds of mankind.

The alienation of modern man with all its consequences makes it difficult for him to solve these problems. Because of the fact that he worships things and has lost the reverence for life, his own and that of his fellow men, he is blind not only to moral principles, but also to rational thought in the interest of his survival. It is clear that atomic armament is likely to lead to universal destruction and, even if atomic war could be prevented, that it will lead to a climate of fear, suspicion, and regimentation which is exactly the climate in which freedom and democracy cannot live. It is clear that the economic gap between poor and rich nations will lead to violent explosions and dictatorships—yet nothing but the most half-hearted and hence futile attempts are suggested to solve these problems. Indeed, it seems that we are going to prove that the gods blind those whom they want to destroy.

Thus far goes the record of capitalism. What is the record of socialism? What did it intend and what did it achieve in those countries in which it had a chance of being realized?

Socialism in the nineteenth century, in the Marxian form and in its many other forms, wanted to create the material basis for a dignified human existence for everybody. It wanted work to direct capital, rather than capital to direct work. For socialism, work and capital were not just two economic categories, but rather they represented two principles: capital, the principle of amassed things, of *having;* and work, that of life and of man's powers, of *being* and becoming. Socialists found that in capitalism things direct life; that *having* is superior to *being;* that the past directs the present—and they wanted to reverse this relation. The aim of socialism was man's emancipation, his restoration to the unalienated, uncrippled individual who enters into a new, rich, spontaneous relationship with his fellow man and with nature. The aim of socialism was that man should throw away the chains which bind him, the fictions and unrealities, and transform himself into a being who can make creative use of his powers of feeling and of thinking. Socialism wanted man to become independent, that is, to stand on his own feet; and it believed that man can stand on his feet only if, as Marx said, "he owes his existence to himself, if he affirms his individuality as a total man in each of his relations to the world, seeing, hearing, smelling, tasting, feeling, thinking, willing, loving—in short, if he affirms and expresses all organs of his individuality." The aim of socialism was the union between man and man, and between man and nature.

Quite in contrast to the frequently uttered cliché that Marx and other socialists taught that the desire for maximal material gain was the most fundamental human drive, these socialists believed that it is the very structure of capitalist society which makes material interest the deepest motive, and that socialism would permit nonmaterial motives to assert themselves and free man from his servitude to material interests. (It is a sad commentary on man's capacity for inconsistency that people condemn socialism for its alleged "materialism," and at the same time criticize it with the argument that only the "profit motive" can motivate man to do his best.)

The aim of socialism was individuality, not uniformity; liberation from economic bonds, not making material aims the main concern of life; the experience of full solidarity of all men, not the manipulation and domination of one man by another. The principle of socialism was that each man is an end in himself and must never be the means of another man. Socialists wanted to create a society in which each citizen actively and responsibly participated in all decisions, and in which a citizen could participate because he was a person and not a thing, because he had convictions and not synthetic opinions.

For socialism not only is poverty a vice, but also wealth. Material poverty deprives man of the basis for a humanly rich life. Material wealth, like power, corrupts man. It destroys the sense of proportion and of the limitations which are inherent in human existence; it creates an unrealistic and almost crazy sense of the "uniqueness" of an individual, making him feel that he is not subject to the same basic conditions of existence as his fellow men. Socialism wants material comfort to be used for the true aims of living; it rejects individual wealth as a danger to society as well as to the individual. In fact, its opposition to capitalism is related to this very principle. By its very logic, capitalism aims at an ever-increasing material wealth, while socialism aims at an ever-increasing human productivity, aliveness, and happiness, and at material comfort only to the extent to which it is conducive to its human aims.

Socialism hoped for the eventual abolition of the state so that only things, and not people, would be administered. It aimed at a classless society in which freedom and initiative would be restored to the individual. Socialism, in the nineteenth century and until the beginning of the First World War, was the most significant humanistic and spiritual movement in Europe and America.

What happened to socialism?

It succumbed to the spirit of capitalism which it had wanted to replace. Instead of understanding it as a movement for the liberation of man, many of its adherents and its enemies alike understood it as being exclusively a movement for the economic improvement of the working class. The humanistic aims of socialism were forgotten, or only paid lip service to, while, as in capitalism, all the emphasis was laid on the aims of economic gain. Just as the ideals of democracy lost their spiritual roots, the idea of socialism lost its deepest root—the prophetic-messianic faith in peace, justice, and the brotherhood of man.

Thus socialism became the vehicle for the workers to attain their place *within* the capitalistic structure rather than transcending it; instead of changing capitalism, socialism was absorbed by its spirit. The failure of the socialist movement became complete when in 1914 its leaders renounced international solidarity and chose the econòmic and military interests of their respective countries as against the ideas of internationalism and peace which had been their program.

The misinterpretation of socialism as a purely economic movement, and of nationalization of the means of production as its principal aim, occurred both in the right wing and in the left wing of the socialist movement. The reformist leaders of the socialist movement in Europe considered it their primary aim to elevate the economic status of the worker within the capitalist system, and they considered as their most radical measures the nationalization of certain big industries. Only recently have many realized that the nationalization of an enterprise is in itself not the realization of socialism, that to be managed by a publicly appointed bureaucracy is not basically different for the worker than being managed by a privately appointed bureaucracy.

The leaders of the Communist Party in the Soviet Union interpreted socialism in the same purely economic way. But living in a country much less developed than western Europe and without a democratic tradition, they applied terror and dictatorship to enforce the rapid accumulation of capital, which in western Europe had occurred in the nineteenth century. They developed a new form of state capitalism which proved to be economically successful and humanly destructive. They built a bureaucratically managed society in which class distinction—both in an economic sense and as far as the power to command others is concerned—is deeper and more rigid than in any of the capitalist societies of today. They define their system as socialistic because they have nationalized the whole economy, while in reality their system is the complete negation of all that socialism stands for—the affirmation of individuality and the full development of man. In order to win the support of the masses who had to make unendurable sacrifices for the sake of the fast accumulation of capital, they used socialistic, combined with nationalistic, ideologies and this gained them the grudging cooperation of the governed.

Thus far the free-enterprise system is superior to the communist system because it has preserved one of the greatest achievements of modern man—political freedom—and with it a respect for the dignity and individuality of man, which links us with the fundamental spiritual tradition of humanism. It permits possibilities of criticism and of making proposals for constructive social change which are practically impossible in the Soviet police state. It is to be expected, however, that once the Soviet countries have achieved the same level of economic development that western Europe and the United States have achieved—that is, once they can satisfy the demand for a comfortable life—they will not need terror, but will be able to use the same means of manipulation which are used in the West: suggestion and persuasion. This development will bring about the convergence of twentieth-century capitalism and twentieth-century communism. Both systems are based on industrialization; their goal is ever-increasing economic efficiency and wealth. They are societies run by a managerial class and by professional politicians. They are both thoroughly materialistic in their outlook, regardless of lip service to Christian ideology in the West and secular Messianism in the East. They organize the masses in a centralized system, in large factories, in political mass parties. In both systems, if they go on in the same way, the mass-man, the alienated man—a well-fed, well-clothed, well-entertained automaton-man governed by bureaucrats who have as little a goal as the mass-man has—will replace the creative, thinking, feeling man. *Things* will have the first place, and man will be dead; he will *talk* of freedom and individuality, while he will *be* nothing.

Where do we stand today?

Capitalism and a vulgarized, distorted socialism have brought man to the point where he is in danger of becoming a dehumanized automaton; he is losing his sanity and stands at the point of total self-destruction. Only full awareness of his situation and its dangers and a new vision of a life which can realize the aims of human freedom, dignity, creativity, reason, justice, and solidarity can save us from almost certain decay, loss of freedom, or destruction. We are not forced to choose between a managerial free-enterprise system and a managerial communist system. There is a third solution, that of democratic, humanistic socialism which, based on the original principles of socialism, offers the vision of a new, truly human society.

VI.   Humanist Socialism

On the basis of the general analysis of capitalism, communism, and humanistic socialism, a socialist program must differentiate between three aspects: What are the *principles* underlying the idea of a socialist party? What are the *intermediate goals* of humanistic socialism for the realization of which socialists work? What are the immediate *short-range goals* for which socialists work, as intermediate goals have not yet been achieved?

What are the *principles* which underlie the idea of a humanistic socialism? Every social and economic system is not only a specific system of relations *between things and institutions,* but a system of *human relations.* Any concept and practice of socialism must be examined in terms of the kind of relations between human beings to which it is conducive.

The supreme value in all social and economic arrangements is man; the goal of society is to offer the conditions for the full development of man's potentialities, his reason, his love, his creativity; all social arrangements must be conducive to overcoming the alienation and crippledness of man, and to enable him to achieve real freedom and individuality. The aim of socialism is an association in which the full development of each is the condition for the full development of all.

The supreme principle of socialism is that man takes precedence over things, life over property, and hence, work over capital; that power follows creation, and not possession; that man must not be governed by circumstances, but circumstances must be governed by man.

In relations between people, every man is an end in himself and must never be made into a means to another man's ends. From this principle it follows that nobody must personally be subject to anyone because he owns capital.

Humanistic socialism is rooted in the conviction of the unity of mankind and the solidarity of all men. It fights any kind of worship of State, nation, or class. The supreme loyalty of man must be to the human race and to the moral principles of humanism. It strives for the revitalization of those ideas and values upon which Western civilization was built.

Humanistic socialism is radically opposed to war and violence in all and any forms. It considers any attempt to solve political and social problems by force and violence not only as futile, but as immoral and inhuman. Hence it is uncompromisingly opposed to any policy which tries to achieve security by armament. It considers peace to be not only the absence of war, but a positive principle of human relations based on free cooperation of all men for the common good.

From socialist principles it follows not only that each member of society feels responsible for his fellow citizens, but for all citizens of the world. The injustice which lets two-thirds of the human race live in abysmal poverty must be removed by an effort far beyond the ones hitherto made by wealthy nations to help the underdeveloped nations to arrive at a humanly satisfactory economic level.

Humanistic socialism stands for freedom. It stands for

freedom from fear, want, oppression, and violence. But freedom is not only *from*, but also freedom *to;* freedom to participate actively and responsibly in all decisions concerning the citizen, freedom to develop the individual's human potential to the fullest possible degree.

Production and consumption must be subordinated to the needs of man's development, not the reverse. As a consequence all production must be directed by the principle of its social usefulness, and not by that of its material profit for some individuals or corporations. Hence if a choice has to be made between greater production on the one hand, and greater freedom and human growth on the other, the human as against the material value must be chosen.

In socialist industrialism the goal is not to achieve the highest *economic* productivity, but to achieve the highest *human* productivity. This means that the way in which man spends most of his energy, in work as well as in leisure, must be meaningful and interesting to him. It must stimulate and help to develop *all* his human powers—his intellectual as well as his emotional and artistic ones.

While, in order to live humanly, basic material needs must be satisfied, consumption must not be an aim in itself. All attempts to stimulate material needs artificially for the sake of profit must be prevented. Waste of material resources and senseless consumption for consumption's sake are destructive to mature human development.

Humanistic socialism is a system in which man governs capital, not capital man; in which, so far as it is possible, man governs his circumstances, not circumstances man; in which the members of society plan what they want to produce, rather than have their production follow the laws of the impersonal powers of the market and of capital with its inherent need for maximum profit.

Humanistic socialism is the extension of the democratic process beyond the purely political realm, into the economic sphere; it is political *and* industrial democracy. It is the restoration of political democracy to its original meaning: the true participation of informed citizens in all decisions affecting them.

Extension of democracy into the economic sphere means democratic control of all economic activities by the participants: manual workers, engineers, administrators, etc. Humanistic socialism is not primarily concerned with legal ownership, but with social control of the large and powerful industries. Irresponsible control by bureaucratic management representing the profit interest of capital must be replaced by administration acting on behalf of, and controlled by, those who produce and consume.

The aim of humanistic socialism can be attained only by the introduction of a maximum of decentralization compatible with a minimum of centralization necessary for the coordinated functioning of an industrial society. The functions of a centralized state must be reduced to a minimum, while the voluntary activity of freely cooperating citizens constitutes the central mechanism of social life.

While the basic general aims of humanistic socialism are the same for all countries, each country must formulate its own specific aims in terms of its own traditional and present situation, and devise its own methods to achieve this aim. The mutual solidarity of socialist countries must exclude any attempt on the part of one country to impose its methods on another. In the same spirit, the writings of the fathers of socialist ideas must not be transformed into sacred scriptures which are used by some to wield authority over others; the spirit common to them, however, must remain alive in the hearts of socialists and guide their thinking.

Humanistic socialism is the voluntary, logical outcome of the operation of human nature under rational conditions. It is the realization of democracy, which has its roots in the humanistic tradition of mankind, under the conditions of an industrial society. It is a social system which operates without force, neither physical force nor that of hypnoid suggestions by which men are forced without being aware of it. It can be achieved only by appealing to man's reason, and to his longing for a more human, meaningful, and rich life. It is based on faith in man's ability to build a world which is truly human, in which the enrichment of life and the unfolding of the individual are the prime objects of society, while economics is reduced to its proper role as the means to a humanly richer life.

In discussing the goals of humanistic socialism we must differentiate between the *final* socialist goal of a society based on the free cooperation of its citizens and the reduction of centralized State activity to a minimum, and the *intermediate* socialist goals before this final aim is reached. The transition from the present centralized State to a completely decentralized form of society cannot be made without a transitory period in which a certain amount of central planning and State intervention will be indispensable. But in order to avoid the dangers that central planning and State intervention may lead to, such as increased bureaucratization and weakening of individual integrity and initiative, it is necessary: a) that the State is brought under the efficient control of its citizens; b) that the social and political power of the big corporations is broken; c) that from the very beginning all forms of decentralized, voluntary associations in production, trade, and local social and cultural activities are promoted.

While it is not possible today to make concrete and detailed plans for the final socialist goals, it is possible to formulate in a tentative fashion the intermediate goals for a socialist society. But even as far as these intermediate goals are concerned, it will take many years of study and experimentation to arrive at more definite and specific formulations, studies to which the best brains and hearts of the nation must be devoted.

Following the principle that social control and not legal ownership is the essential principle of socialism, its first goal is the transformation of all big enterprises in such a way that their administrators are appointed and fully controlled by all participants—workers, clerks, engineers—with the participation of trade union and consumer representatives. These groups constitute the highest authority for every big enterprise. They decide all basic questions of production, price, utilization of profits, etc. The stockholders continue to receive an appropriate compensation for the use of their capital, but have no right of control and administration.

The autonomy of an enterprise is restricted by central planning to the extent to which it is necessary to make production serve its social ends.

Small enterprises should work on a cooperative basis, and they are to be encouraged by taxation and other means. Inasmuch as they do not work on a cooperative basis, the participants must share in the profits and control the administration on an equal basis with the owner.

Certain industries which are of basic importance for the whole of society, such as oil, banking, television, radio, medical drugs, and transportation, must be nationalized; but the administration of these nationalized industries must follow the same principles of effective control by participants, unions and consumers.

In all fields in which there is a social need but not an adequate existing production, society must finance enterprises which serve these needs.

The individual must be protected from fear and the need to submit to anyone's coercion. In order to accomplish this aim, society must provide, free for everyone, the minimum necessities of material existence in food, housing, and clothing. Anyone who has higher aspirations for material comforts will have to work for them, but the minimal necessities of life being guaranteed, no person can have power over anyone on the basis of direct or indirect material coercion.

Socialism does not do away with individual property for use. Neither does it require the complete leveling of income; income should be related to effort and skill. But differences in income should not create such different forms of material life that the life experience of one cannot be shared by, and thus remains alien to, another.

The principle of political democracy must be implemented in terms of the twentieth-century reality. Considering our technical instrumentalities of communication and tabulation, it is possible to reintroduce the principle of the town meeting into contemporary mass society. The forms in which this can be accomplished need study and experimentation. They may consist of the formation of hundreds of thousands of small face-to-face groups (organized along the principle of place of work or place of residence) which would constitute a new type of Lower House, sharing decision-making with a centrally elected parliament. Decentralization must strive at putting important decisions into the hands of the inhabitants of small, local areas which are still subject to the fundamental principles which govern the life of the whole society. But whichever forms are to be found, the essential principle is that the democratic process is transformed into one in which well-informed and responsible citizens—not automatized mass-men, controlled by the methods of hypnoid mass suggestion—express their will.

Not only in the sphere of political decisions, but with regard to all decisions and arrangements, the grip of the bureaucracy must be broken in order to restore freedom. Aside from decisions which filter down from above, activity in all spheres of life on the grass-roots level must be developed which can "filter up" from below to the top. Workers organized in unions, consumers organized in consumers' organizations, citizens organized in the above-mentioned face-to-face political units, must be in constant interchange with central authorities. This interchange must be such that new measures, laws, and provisions can be suggested and, after voting, decided from the grass roots, and that all elected representatives are subject to continuous critical appraisal and, if necessary, recall.

According to its basic principles, the aim of socialism is the abolition of national sovereignty, the abolition of any kind of armed forces, and the establishment of a commonwealth of nations.

In the sphere of education, the main aims are those of helping to develop the critical powers of the individual and to provide a basis for the creative expression of his personality—in other words, to nurture free men who will be immune to manipulation and to the exploitation of their suggestibility for the pleasure and profit of others. Knowledge should not be a mere mass of information, but the rational means of understanding the underlying forces that determine material and human processes. Education should embrace not only reason but the arts. Capitalism, as it has produced alienation, has divorced and debased both man's scientific understanding and his aesthetic perception. The aim of socialist education is to restore man to the full and free exercise of both. It seeks to make man not only an intelligent spectator but a well-equipped participant, not only in the production of material goods, but in the enjoyment of life. To offset the dangers of alienated intellectualization, factual and theoretical instruction shall be supplemented by training in manual work and in the creative arts, combining the two in craftsmanship (the production of useful objects of art), in primary and secondary education. Each adolescent must have had the experience of producing something valuable with his own hands and skills.

The principle of irrational authority based on power and exploitation must be replaced, not by a laissez-faire attitude, but by an authority which is based on the competence of knowledge and skill—not on intimidation, force, or suggestion. Socialist education must arrive at a new concept of rational authority which differs both from irrational authoritarianism and from an unprincipled laissez-faire attitude.

Education must not be restricted to childhood and adolescence, but the existing forms of adult education must be greatly enlarged. It is especially important to give each person the possibility of changing his occupation or profession at any time of life; this will be economically possible if at least his minimal material needs are taken care of by society.

Cultural activities must not be restricted to providing intellectual education. All forms of artistic expression (through music, dance, drama, painting, sculpture, architecture, etc.) are of paramount importance for the human development of man. Society must channel considerable means for the creation of a vast program of artistic activities and useful as well as beautiful building programs, even at the expense of other and less important consumer satisfactions. Great care should be taken, however, to conserve the integrity of the creative artist, to avoid turning socially responsible art into bureaucratic or "State" art. A healthy balance must be maintained between the legitimate claims of the artist upon society and its legitimate claims upon him. Socialism seeks to narrow the gap between the producer and the consumer in the realm of art and seeks ultimately to eliminate this distinction so far as possible by creating optimum conditions for the flourishing of every individual's creative potentialities. But it holds up no preconceived pattern and recognizes that this is a problem that will require much more study than has been given to it up till now.

Complete equality of races and sexes is a matter of course for a socialist society. This equality, however, does not imply sameness, and every effort must be made to permit the fullest development of the gifts and talents peculiar to each racial and national group, as well as to the two sexes.

Freedom of religious activities must be guaranteed, together with the complete separation of State and Church.

The foregoing program is meant to serve as a guide to the principles and goals of socialism. Its concrete and detailed formulation requires a great deal of discussion. To conduct this discussion and to arrive at concrete and detailed suggestions is one of the main tasks of a socialist party.

Such discussion requires examining all data which practical experience and the social sciences can bring forward. But first of all it requires imagination and the courage to see new possibilities, instead of the outworn routine of thinking.

Quite aside from this, it will take considerable time until the majority of the people in the United States will be convinced of the validity of socialist principles and goals. What is the task and function of a socialist party during the time before it has succeeded in this task?

The SP-SDF (Socialist Party–Social Democratic Federation) must embody in its own structure and activities the very principles it stands for; it must not only strive for the achievement of socialism in the future, but must begin with its realization in its own midst immediately. Hence the SP-SDF must not try to convince the people of its program by appeal to irrational emotions, hypnoid suggestions, or "attractive personalities," but by the realism, correctness, and penetration of its analysis of economic, social, political, and human situations. The SP-SDF must become the moral and intellectual conscience of the United States and divulge its analyses and judgments in the widest possible manner.

The conduct of activities of the SP-SDF must follow its principles in the sense of the optimum of decentralization and the active, responsible participation of its members in discussions and decisions. It must also give full scope to the expression and divulgence of minority opinions. The socialist program cannot be a fixed plan, but must grow and develop through the continuous activity, effort, and concern of the members of the party.

The SP-SDF thus must be different from other political parties, not only in its program and ideals, but in its very structure and way of functioning. It must become a spiritual and social home for all its members who are united in the spirit of humanistic realism and sanity, and by the solidarity of the common concern for and the common faith in man and his future.

The SP-SDF must develop an extensive educational campaign among workers, students, professionals, and members of all social classes who can be expected to have a potential understanding for socialist criticism and socialist ideals.

The SP-SDF cannot expect to gain victory in a short time. But this does not mean that it should not aim at the widest social influence and power. It must strive to gain the allegiance of an ever-increasing number of people who, through the party, make their voices heard within the United States and throughout the whole world.

The SP-SDF is rooted in the humanistic tradition of socialism; it strives for the transformation of the traditional socialist goals to fit the conditions of twentieth-century society as a condition for their realization. Particularly it rejects the ideas of achieving its goals by force or by the establishment of any kind of dictatorship. Its only weapons are the realism of its ideas, the fact that they appeal to the true needs of man, and the enthusiastic allegiance which those citizens will give it who have seen through the fictions and delusions which fill the minds of people today, and who have faith in a richer, fuller life.

It is not enough that the members of the SP-SDF believe in a common ideal. Such faith becomes empty and sterile if it is not translated into action. The life of the party must be organized in such a manner that it offers ample and varied possibility for every member to translate his concern into meaningful and immediate action. How can this be done?

It must be understood clearly that the basic goals of socialism, especially the method of management of big enterprises by the participants, union and consumers' representatives, the revitalization of the democratic process, the guaranteed minimum for existence for every citizen, constitute problems the details of which are exceedingly difficult to solve. Their solution requires basic theoretical research in the fields of economics, work organization, psychology, etc.; and, in addition, it requires practical plans and experimentation. If these social problems are approached in the same spirit of faith and imagination which exists among the natural scientists and technicians, solutions will be found which, looked at from the present situation, might appear as fantastic as space travel appeared twenty years ago. Yet the difficulties of arriving at a solution for a sane and human social organization are not any greater than those in the fields of the theoretical and applied natural sciences.

The first task, then, for socialists is to study the problems of applied socialism within their own sphere of activity and to discuss their experiences and suggestions for socialist solutions in the working units of their SP-SDF. Supplementing this group activity are permanent committees for the investigation of these problems. These committees will be composed of specialists in the various fields of economics, sociology, psychology, foreign policy, etc. The committees of investigation and the working units will be in close mutual contact, exchanging their ideas and experiences, and thus stimulating each other.

But the activities of the members of the SP-SDF must not be restricted to imaginative thinking and planning. Beyond this, immediate and concrete action is necessary. It is important that each member demonstrates the socialist way of life in his or her place of work, wherever it may be—in factories, offices, schools, laboratories, hospitals, etc. Each member must demonstrate the socialist way of approaching problems by his own way of dealing with them and by stimulating others. It is especially important that the members of the SP-SDF who are union members work actively for greater member activity and participation in the life of the trade unions. Inside and outside the trade unions, the members of the SP-SDF will support all tendencies for decentralization, active grass-roots participation, and fight all forms of bureaucratism.

The SP-SDF wants to attract men and women who are genuinely concerned with the problem of the humanization of society and who, out of this concern, work for it and are willing to make the sacrifice in time and money which this work requires.

Although the SP-SDF has its center in the fundamental goals of its programs, it will participate actively in the furtherance of all immediate political aims which are of importance for the progressive development of our society. It will cooperate with all political groupings and individuals that sincerely strive for the same aims. Among these aims are, in particular:

• A sane foreign policy, based on a realistic appreciation of the given facts of political life—a policy which seeks reasonable compromise and realizes that war can be averted only if the two power blocs accept their present economic and political positions and renounce every attempt to change them by force.

• Fight against the idea that our security can be gained by armaments. The only way to avoid total destruction lies in total disarmament. This implies that disarmament negotiations must not be used to prevent real disarmament, but that we must be willing to take risks in the attempt to achieve it.

• A program of economic aid to underdeveloped countries on an immensely larger scale than our present one, and at the cost of considerable sacrifice on the part of our citizens for the accomplishment of such a program. We advocate a policy which does not serve the interests of American capital investments in foreign countries and does not involve United States foreign policy in indirect interference with the independence of small nations.

• Strengthening of the United Nations and of all efforts to use its assistance in the solving of international disputes and in large-scale foreign aid.

• Support of all measures to raise the standard of living of that part of our population which is still living below the material standard of the majority. This applies to poverty caused by economic as well as by regional and racial factors.

• Support of all efforts for decentralization and grass-roots activities. This implies support of all attempts to curb irresponsible power in corporate, governmental, and union bureaucracy.

• Support of all measures for social security which lead to immediate relief in distress situations caused by unemployment, sickness, and old age. Support of all measures in the direction of socialized medicine, with the understanding that the free choice of doctors and a high level of medical services must be upheld.

• Economic measures which lead to the full use of our agricultural productive capacity and our surplus, nationally and internationally.

• Support of measures to set up an economic commission consisting of representatives of industry, commerce, trade unions, economists, and consumer representatives. This commission should be charged with undertaking a regular examination of the needs of our economy and developing overall plans for changes in the interest of the nation as a whole. Its most immediate task would be to discuss and propose plans for the change from armaments to peace production. The reports of this commission, including minority reports, should be published and distributed widely. Similar commissions should be convoked in the field of foreign policy, culture, and education; the members of these commissions should represent wide sectors of the population, and consist of men whose knowledge and integrity are generally recognized.

• Vast governmental expenditures for housing, road building, and hospital construction, and for cultural activities such as music, theater, dance, and art.

• Given the wealth of the United States, we can begin to experiment socially. State-owned enterprises must be organized in which various forms of workers' participation in management are tried out.

• In industries of basic social importance, the government

must organize yardstick enterprises, which compete with private industry and in this way force it to raise its standards. This must be done first of all in the field of radio, television and movies, and in other fields if desirable.

• Efforts must be made to begin with a program of workers' participation in the management of the big corporations. Twenty-five percent of the votes on the decision-making boards should be given to workers and employees, freely elected in each enterprise.

• The influence of the unions must be strengthened, not only with regard to the problems of wages, but also with regard to their influence on problems of working conditions, etc. Simultaneously a process of democratization within the unions must be furthered with all energy.

• All attempts must be supported which aim at the restriction of hypnoid suggestion in commercial and political propaganda.

We are aware that the above-mentioned program refers mainly to industrialized countries like those of North America and Europe. For all other countries the program must vary according to their specific conditions. However, the general principles underlying this program, that of production for social use, the strengthening of an effective democratic process, industrially as well as politically, are valid for all countries.

We appeal to every citizen to feel his responsibility for his life, that of his children and that of the whole human family. Man is on the verge of the most crucial choice he has ever made: whether to use his skill and brain to create a world which can be, if not a paradise, at least a place for the fullest realization of man's potentialities, a world of joy and creativity—or a world which will destroy itself either with atomic bombs or through boredom and emptiness.

Indeed, socialism differs from other party programs in that it has a vision, an ideal for a better, more human society than the present one. Socialism does not want only to improve this or that defect of capitalism, it wants to accomplish something which does not yet exist; it aims at a goal which transcends the given empirical social reality, yet which is based on a real potentiality. Socialists have a vision and say: this is what we want; this is what we strive for; it is not the absolute and the final form of life, but it is a much better, more human form of life. It is the realization of the ideals of humanism which have inspired the greatest achievements of Western and Eastern culture.

Many will say that people do not want ideals, that they do not want to go beyond the frame of reference in which they live. We socialists say that this is not true. On the contrary, people have a deep longing for something they can work for and have faith in. Man's whole vitality depends on the fact that he transcends the routine part of his existence, that he strives for the fulfillment of a vision which is not impossible to realize—even though it has not yet been achieved. If he has no chance to strive for a rational, humanistic vision, he will eventually, worn out and depressed by the boredom of his life, fall prey to the irrational satanic visions of dictators and demagogues. It is exactly the weakness of contemporary society that it offers no ideals, that it demands no faith, that it has no vision—except that of more of the same. We socialists are not ashamed to confess that we have a deep faith in man and in a vision of a new, human form of society. We appeal to the faith, hope and imagination of our fellow citizens to join us in this vision and in the attempt to realize it. Socialism is not only a socioeconomic and political program; it is a human program: *the realization of the ideals of humanism under the conditions of an industrial society.*

Socialism must be radical. To be radical is to go to the roots; and the root is Man.

VII. The Psychological Aspects of the Guaranteed Income

This paper focuses exclusively on the *psychological* aspects of the guaranteed income, its value, its risks, and the human problems it raises.

The most important reason for the acceptance of the concept is that it might drastically enhance the freedom of the individual.[1] Until now in human history, man has been limited in his freedom to act by two factors: the use of force on the part of the rulers (essentially their capacity to kill the dissenters), and, more importantly, the threat of starvation against all who were unwilling to accept the conditions of work and social existence that were imposed on them.

Whoever was not willing to accept these conditions, even if there was no other force used against him, was confronted with the threat of starvation. The principle prevailing throughout most of human history in the past and present (in capitalism as well as in the Soviet Union) is: "He who does not work shall not eat." This threat forced man not only to *act* in accordance with what was demanded of him, but also to *think* and to *feel* in such a way that he would not even be tempted to act differently.

The fact that past history is based on the principle of the

threat of starvation has, in the last analysis, its source in the fact that, with the exception of certain primitive societies, man has lived on the level of scarcity, both economically and psychologically. There were never sufficient material goods to satisfy the needs of all; usually a small group of "directors" took for themselves all that their hearts desired, and the many who could not sit at the table were told that it was God's or Nature's law that this should be so. But it must be noted that the main factor in this is not the greed of the "directors," but the low level of material productivity.

A guaranteed income, which becomes possible in the era of economic abundance, could for the first time free man from the threat of starvation, and thus make him truly free and independent from any economic threat. Nobody would have to accept conditions of work merely because he otherwise would be afraid of starving; a talented or ambitious man or woman could learn new skills to prepare himself or herself for a different kind of occupation. A woman could leave her husband, an adolescent his family. People would learn to be no longer afraid, if they did not have to fear hunger. (This holds true, of course, only if there is also no political threat that inhibits man's free thought, speech, and action.)

Guaranteed income would not only establish freedom as a reality rather than a slogan, it would also establish a principle deeply rooted in Western religious and humanist tradition: man has the right to live, regardless! This right to live, to have food, shelter, medical care, education, etc., is an intrinsic human right that cannot be restricted by any condition, not even the one that he must be socially "useful."

The shift from a psychology of scarcity to that of abundance is one of the most important steps in human development. A psychology of scarcity produces anxiety, envy, egotism (to be seen most drastically in peasant cultures all over the world). A psychology of abundance produces initiative, faith in life, solidarity. The fact is that most men are still geared psychologically to the economic facts of scarcity, when the industrial world is in the process of entering a new era of economic abundance. But because of this psychological "lag" many people cannot even understand new ideas as presented in the concept of a guaranteed income, because traditional ideas are usually determined by feelings that originated in previous forms of social existence.

A further effect of a guaranteed income, coupled with greatly diminished working hours for all, would be that the spiritual and religious problems of human existence would become real and imperative. Until now man has been occupied with work (or has been too tired after work) to be too seriously concerned with such problems as "What is the meaning of life?" "What do I believe in?" "What are my values?" "Who am I?" etc. If he ceases to be mainly occupied by work, he will either be free to confront these problems seriously, or he will become half mad from direct or compensated boredom.

From all this it would follow that economic abundance, liberation from fear of starvation, would mark the transition from a prehuman to a truly human society.

Balancing this picture, it is necessary to raise some objections against, or questions about, the concept of a guaranteed income. The most obvious question is whether a guaranteed income would not reduce the incentive for work.

Aside from the fact that there is already no work for an ever-increasing sector of the population, and hence that the question of incentive for these people is irrelevant, the objection is nevertheless a serious one. I believe, however, that it can be demonstrated that material incentive is by no means the only incentive for work and effort. First of all there are other incentives: pride, social recognition, pleasure in work itself, etc. Examples of this fact are not lacking. The most obvious one to quote is the work of scientists, artists, etc., whose outstanding achievements were not motivated by the incentive of monetary profit, but by a mixture of various factors: most of all, interest in the work they were doing; also pride in their achievements, or the wish for fame. But obvious as this example may seem, it is not entirely convincing, because it can be said that these outstanding people could make extraordinary efforts precisely because they were extraordinarily gifted, and hence they are no example for the reactions of the average person. This objection does not seem to be valid, however, if we consider the incentives for the activities of people who do not share the outstanding qualities of the great creative persons. What efforts are made in the field of all sports, of many kinds of hobbies, where there are no material incentives of any kind! To what extent interest in the work process itself can be an incentive for working was clearly demonstrated for the first time by Professor Mayo in his classic study at the Chicago Hawthorne Works of the Western Electric Company.[2] The very fact that unskilled women workers were drawn into the experiment of work productivity of which they were the subjects, the fact that they became interested and active participants in the experiment, resulted in increased productivity, and even their physical health improved.

The problem becomes even clearer when we consider older forms of societies. The efficiency and incorruptibility of the traditional Prussian civil service were famous, in spite of the fact that monetary rewards were very low; in this case such concepts as honor, loyalty, duty, were the determining motivations for efficient work. Still another factor appears when we consider preindustrial societies (like the medieval European society, or half-feudal societies in the beginning of this century in Latin America). In these societies the carpenter, for instance, wanted to earn enough to satisfy the needs of his traditional standard of living, and would refuse to work more in order to earn more than he needed.

Secondly, it is a fact that man, by nature, is not lazy, but on the contrary, suffers from the results of inactivity. People might prefer not to work for one or two months, but the vast majority would beg to work, even if they were not paid for it. The fields of child development and mental illness offer abundant data in this connection; what is needed is a systematic investigation in which the available data are organized and analyzed from the standpoint of "laziness as disease," and more data are collected in new and pertinent investigations.

However, if money is not to be the main incentive, then work in its technical or social aspects would have to be sufficiently attractive and interesting to outweigh the unpleasure of inactivity. Modern, alienated man is deeply bored (usually unconsciously) and hence has a yearning for laziness, rather than for activity. This yearning itself is, however, a symptom of our "pathology of normalcy." Presumably misuse of the guaranteed income would disappear after a short time, just as people would not overeat on sweets after a few weeks, assuming they would not have to pay for them.

Another objection is the following: Will the disappearance of the fear of starvation really make man so much freer, considering that those who earn a comfortable living are probably just as afraid to lose a job that gives them, let us say, $15,000 a year, as are those who might go hungry if they were to lose their jobs? If this objection is valid, then the guaranteed income would increase the freedom of the large majority, but not that of the middle and upper classes.

In order to understand this objection fully we have to consider the spirit of contemporary industrial society. Man has transformed himself into a *homo consumens*. He is voracious, passive, and tries to compensate for his inner emptiness by continuous and ever-increasing consumption (there are many clinical examples for this mechanism in cases of overeating, overbuying, overdrinking, as a reaction to depression and anxiety); he consumes cigarettes, liquor, sex, movies, travel, as well as education, books, lectures, and art. He *appears* to be active, "thrilled," yet deep down he is anxious, lonely, depressed, and bored (boredom can be defined as that type of chronic depression that can successfully be compensated by consumption). Twentieth-century industrialism has created this new psychological type, *homo consumens*, primarily for economic reasons, i.e., the need for mass consumption, which is stimulated and manipulated by advertising. But the character type, once created, also influences the economy and makes the principles of ever-increasing satisfaction appear rational and realistic.[3]

Contemporary man has an unlimited hunger for more and more consumption. From this follow several consequences: if there is no limit to the greed for consumption, and since in the foreseeable future no economy can produce enough for unlimited consumption for everybody, there can never be true "abundance" (psychologically speaking) as long as the character structure of *homo consumens* remains dominant. For the greedy person there is always scarcity, since he never has enough, regardless of how much he has. Furthermore he feels covetous and competitive with regard to everybody else; hence he is basically isolated and frightened. He cannot really enjoy art or other cultural stimulations, since he remains basically greedy. This means that those who lived on the guaranteed-income level would feel frustrated and worthless, and those who earned more would remain prisoners of circumstances, because they would be frightened and lose the possibility for maximum consumption. For these reasons I believe that guaranteed income without a change from the principle of maximal consumption would only take care of certain problems (economical and social) but would not have the radical effect it should.

What, then, must be done to implement the guaranteed income? Generally speaking, we must change our system from one of maximal to one of optimal consumption. This would mean:

A vast change in industry from the production of commodities for individual consumption to the production of commodities for public use: schools, theaters, libraries, parks, hospitals, public transportation, housing; in other words an emphasis on the production of those things that are the basis for the unfolding of the individual's inner productiveness and activity. It can be shown that the voraciousness of *homo consumens* refers mainly to the individual consumption of things he "eats" (incorporates), while the use of free public services, enabling the individual to enjoy life, do not evoke greed and voraciousness. Such a change from maximal to optimal consumption would require drastic changes in production patterns, and also a drastic reduction of the appetite-whetting, brainwashing techniques of advertising, etc.[4] It would also have to be combined with a drastic cultural change: a renaissance of the humanistic value of life, productivity, individualism, etc., as against the materialism of the "organization man" and manipulated ant heaps.

These considerations lead to other problems that need to be studied: Are there objectively valid criteria to distinguish between rational and irrational, between good and bad needs, or is any subjectively felt need of the same value? (Good is defined here as needs that enhance human aliveness, awakeness, productivity, sensitivity; bad, as those needs that weaken or paralyze these human potentials.) It must be remembered that in the case of drug addiction, overeating, alcoholism, we all make such a distinction. The study of these problems would lead to the following practical considerations: what are the minimum legitimate needs of an individual? (For instance: one room per person, so much clothing, so many calories, so many culturally valuable commodities such as a radio, books, etc.) In a relatively abundant society such as that of the United States today, it should be easy to figure out what the cost for a *decent* subsistence minimum is, and also what the limits for maximal consumption should be. Progressive taxation on consumption beyond a certain threshold could be considered. It seems important to me that slum conditions should be avoided. All this would mean the combination of the principles of a guaranteed income with the transformation of our society from maximal to optimal individual consumption, and a drastic shift from production for individual needs to production for public needs.

I believe it is important to add to the idea of a guaranteed income another one, which ought to be studied: the concept of *free* consumption of certain commodities. One example would be that of bread, then milk, and vegetables. Let us assume, for a moment, that everyone could go into any bakery and take as much bread as he liked (the state would pay the bakery for all bread produced). As already mentioned, the greedy would at first take more than they could use, but after a short time this "greed-consumption" would even itself out and people would take only what they really needed. Such free consumption would, in my opinion, create a new dimension in human life (unless we look at it as the repetition on a much higher level of the consumption pattern in certain primitive societies). Man would be freed from the principle "he who does not work shall not eat." Even this beginning of free consumption might constitute a very novel experience of freedom. It is obvious even to the noneconomist that the provision of free bread for all could be easily paid for by the state, which would cover this disbursement by a corresponding tax. However, we can go a step further. Assuming that not only all minimal needs for food were obtained free—bread, milk, vegetables, fruit—but the minimal needs for clothing (by some system everybody could obtain, without paying, say one suit, three shirts, six pairs of socks, etc., per year); that transportation was free, requiring, of course, vastly improved systems of public transportation, while private cars would become more expensive. Eventually one could imagine that housing could be solved in the same way, by big housing projects with sleeping halls for the young, one small room for older, or married couples, to be used without cost by anybody who chose. This leads me to the suggestion that another way of solving the guaranteed-income problem would be by free minimal consumption of all necessities, instead of through cash payments. The production of these minimum necessities, together with highly improved public services, would keep production going, just as guaranteed-income payments would.

It may be objected that this method is more radical, and hence less acceptable, than the one proposed by the other authors. This is probably true; but it must not be forgotten that, on the one hand, this method of free minimal services could theoretically be arranged within the present system while on the other hand, the idea of a guaranteed income will not be acceptable to many, not because it is not feasible, but because of the psychological resistance against the abolishment of the principle "He who does not work shall not eat."

One other philosophical, political, and psychological problem has to be studied: that of freedom. The Western concept of freedom was to a large extent based on the freedom to own property, and to exploit it, as long as other legitimate interests were not threatened. This principle has actually been punctured in many ways in Western industrial societies by taxation, which is a form of expropriation, and by state intervention in agriculture, trade, and industry. At the same time, private property in the means of production is becoming increasingly replaced by the semi-public property typical of giant corporations. While the guaranteed-income concept would mean some additional state regulations, it must be remembered that today the concept of freedom for the average individual lies not so much in the freedom to own and exploit property (capital) as in the freedom to consume whatever he likes. Many people today consider it as an interference with their freedom if unlimited consumption is restricted, although only those on top are really free to choose what they want. The competition between different brands of the same commodities and different kinds of commodities creates the illusion of personal freedom, when in reality the individual wants what he is conditioned to want.[5] A new approach to the problem of freedom is necessary, only with the transformation of *homo consumens* into a productive, active person will man experience freedom in true independence and not in unlimited choice of commodities.

The full effect of the principle of the guaranteed income is to be expected only in conjunction with: (1) a change in habits of consumption, the transformation of *homo consumens* into the productive, active man (in Spinoza's sense); (2) the creation of a new spiritual attitude, that of humanism (in theistic or nontheistic forms); and (3) a renaissance of truly democratic methods (for instance, a new Lower House by the integration and summation of decisions arrived at by hundreds of thousands of face-to-face groups, active participation of all members working in any kind of enterprise, in management, etc.).[6] The danger that a state that nourishes all could become a mother goddess with dictatorial qualities can be overcome only by a simultaneous, drastic increase in democratic procedure in all spheres of social activities. (The fact is that even today the state is extremely powerful, without giving these benefits.)

In sum, together with economic research in the field of the guaranteed income, other research must be undertaken: psychological, philosophical, religious, educational. The great step of a guaranteed income will, in my opinion, succeed only if it is accompanied by changes in other spheres. It must not be forgotten that the guaranteed income can succeed only if we stop spending 10 percent of our total resources on economically useless and dangerous armaments; if we can halt the spread of senseless violence by systematic help to the underdeveloped countries, and if we find methods to arrest the population explosion. Without such changes, no plan for the future will succeed, because there will be no future.

Notes

1. Cf. my discussion of a "universal subsistence guarantee" in *The Sane Society* (New York: Holt, Rinehart and Winston, 1955), pp. 355 ff.

2. Cf. Elton Mayo, *The Human Problem of an Industrial Civilization,* 2nd ed. (New York: The Macmillan Co., 1946).

3. The problem is all the more complicated by the fact that at least 20% of the American population live on a level of scarcity as in some parts of Europe, especially the socialist countries, which have not yet attained a satisfactory standard of living, and that the majority of mankind, which dwells in Latin America, Asia, and Africa, is still living at hardly above starvation level. Any argument for less consumption meets with the argument that in most of the world *more* consumption is needed. This is perfectly true, but the danger exists that even in the countries that are now poor, the ideal of maximal consumption will guide their effort, form their spirit, and hence will continue to be effective even when the level of optimal (not maximal) consumption has been reached.

4. The need of restricting advertising and, even more, of changing production in the direction of greater production of public services are, in my opinion, hardly thinkable without a great deal of state intervention.

5. Here too, the totalitarian bureaucratization of consumption in the Soviet-bloc countries has made a bad case for any regulation of consumption.

6. Cf. Fromm, *The Sane Society,* loc. cit.

VIII.   The Case for Unilateral Disarmament

There is little doubt that the proposal for a unilateral disarmament—in the broad sense of the unconditional dismantling of a country's military establishment—will be acceptable neither to the United States nor to the Soviet Union in the immediate future. Hence, inasmuch as this paper is concerned with *practical* suggestions for arms control, it proposes another and very limited concept of unilateral disarmament, one which has been called by Charles Osgood *"graduated unilateral action (or disengagement)"* or which might be called *unilateral initiative in taking practical steps toward disarmament.* The basic idea underlying this concept is that of a radical change of our method of negotiating multilateral disarmament. This change implies that we give up the present method of bargaining in which every concession we make is dependent on a corresponding and guaranteed concession on the part of the Russians; that, instead, we take, unilaterally, gradual steps toward disarmament in the expectation that the Russians will reciprocate and that, thus, the present deadlock in the negotiations for universal disarmament can be broken through.

In order to describe the nature of this policy of unilateral steps, I cannot improve on the following description by Osgood, who, as far as I know, was the first one to express this idea in two brilliant and profound articles.[1] "To be maximally effective," he writes, "in inducing the enemy to reciprocate, a unilateral act (1) should, in terms of *military aggression,* be clearly disadvantageous to the side making it, yet not cripplingly so; (2) should be such as to be clearly perceived by the enemy as reducing his external threat; (3) should not increase the enemy's threat to our heartland;[2] (4) should be such that reciprocal action by the enemy is clearly available and clearly indicated; (5) should be announced in advance and widely publicized to ally, neutral and enemy countries—as regards the nature of the act, its purpose as part of a consistent policy, and the expected reciprocation; but (6) should not demand prior commitment to reciprocation by the enemy as a condition for its commission."[3]

As to the specific steps which should be taken in this fashion, it would require a great deal of further thought, aided by competent specialists. But in order to give at least an idea of the concrete steps this policy would envisage, I want to mention the following (some of them in agreement with Osgood): sharing of scientific information; stopping of atomic tests; troop reductions; evacuation of one or more military bases; discontinuation of German rearmament; etc. The expectation is that the Russians are as willing as we are to avoid war, hence that they will begin to reciprocate and that once the course of mutual suspicion has been reversed, bigger steps can be taken which may lead to complete bilateral disarmament. Furthermore, I believe that disarmament negotiations should be paralleled by *political* negotiations, which aim essentially at mutual noninterference on the basis of the recognition of the *status quo.* Here, too (and again in essential agreement with Osgood's position), unilateral steps such as the recognition of the Oder-Neisse line and admission of China to the United Nations would be taken in the expectation of reciprocation by the Russians (i.e., curbing of Chinese aggression, noninterference in the Middle and Far East).

What are the premises underlying the proposition for unilateral steps toward disarmament? (At this point I shall mention only some fundamental ones, while others will be discussed in the second part of this paper which presents the argument for total unilateral disarmament.) They are briefly: (1) that, as indicated before, the present method of negotiations does not seem to lead to the goal of bilateral disarmament because of the deeply ingrained mutual suspicions and fears; (2) that without achieving *complete* disarmament, the armament race will continue and lead to the destruction of our civilization as well as that of the Russians or, even without the outbreak of a war, will slowly undermine and eventually destroy the values in defense of which we are risking our physical existence; (3) that while unilateral steps constitute a definite risk (and must be so by the very nature of the idea), the risk at every step is not a crippling one and is infinitely smaller than the danger we run by the continuation of the arms race.

Even though the broader concept of complete—rather than graduated—unilateral disarmament is, as stated before, not a practical possibility in the near future, as far as the United States and the USSR are concerned, I believe it worthwhile to present the arguments for this position, not primarily because the editor of this journal asked me to present this position nor even because I share it with a small minority of others who believe that the risks in the continuation of the armament race are far greater than the very serious risks of unilateral disarmament. While both reasons might not be sufficient to justify the following presentation, I do believe that it is not only justified but important for another reason: thinking through the arguments for a radical—even though practically unacceptable—position contributes to breaking through the thought barrier which prevents us now from getting out of the dangerous circle of seeking peace by means of threat and counterthreat. Taking seriously the reasoning which supports the unpopular position of complete unilateral disarmament can open up new approaches and viewpoints which are important even if our practical aim is that of graduated unilateral action or even only that of negotiated bilateral disarmament. I believe that the difficulty of arriving at complete disarmament lies to a large extent in the frozen stereotypes of feelings and thought habits on both sides and that any attempt at unfreezing these patterns and of rethinking the whole problem can be of importance in finding a way out of the present dangerous impasse.

The proposal for complete unilateral disarmament has been advocated from a religious, moral or pacifist position by such men as Victor Gollancz, Lewis Mumford, and some Quakers. It has also been supported by men like Bertrand Russell, Stephen King-Hall, and C. W. Mills, who are not opposed to the use of force under all or any circumstances, yet who are uncompromisingly opposed both to thermonuclear war and to all and any preparation for it. This writer finds himself somewhat between the position of the strict pacifists and men like Bertrand Russell and Stephen King-Hall.[4]

The difference between these two groups, however, is not as fundamental as it may seem. They are united by their critical attitude toward the irrational aspects of international politics and by their deep reverence for life. They share the conviction of the oneness of the human race and faith in the spiritual and intellectual potentialities of man. They follow the dictates of their conscience in refusing to have any "part in making millions of women and children and noncombatants hostages for the behavior of their own governments."[5] Whether they think in theistic terms or in those of nontheistic humanism (in the sense of the philosophic continuum from Stoic to eighteenth-century Enlightenment philosophy), they all are rooted in the same spiritual tradition and are unwilling to compromise with its principles. They are united by their uncompromising opposition to any kind of idolatry, including the idolatry of the state. While their opposition to the Soviet system is rooted precisely in this attitude against idolatry, they are critical of idolatry whenever it appears in the Western world whether it is in the name of God or of democracy.

While there is no proponent of unilateral disarmament who does not believe that the individual must be willing to give his life for the sake of his supreme values, if such an ultimate necessity arises, they are all equally convinced that to risk the life of the human race, or even the results of its best efforts in the last five thousand years, is immoral and irresponsible. As warfare becomes at once more senseless and more devastating, the convergence between religious pacifist, humanist, and pragmatic opponents to nuclear armament grows.

From the standpoint of the proponents of unilateral disarmament, to continue the armament race is catastrophic, *whether the deterrent works or not.* In the first place, they have little faith that the deterrent will prevent the outbreak of a thermonuclear war.[6] They believe that the results of a thermonuclear war would be such that in the very "best" case they completely belie the idea that we ought to fight such a war in order to save our democratic way of life. There is no need to enter the guessing game as to whether one-third or two-thirds of the population of the two opponents and what proportion of the neutral world (depending on how the wind blows) will be destroyed. This is a guessing game that verges on madness; for to consider the possibility of the destruction of 30%, 60%, or 90% of one's own and the enemy's population as an acceptable (although, of course, most undesirable) result of one's policy is indeed approaching pathology. The increasing split between intellect and affect, which is so characteristic of our Western development in the last centuries, has reached its dangerous, schizoid peak in the calm and allegedly rational way in which we can discuss possible world destruction as a result of our own action. It does not take much imagination to visualize that sudden destruction and the threat of slow death to a large part of the American population, or the Russian population, or large parts of the world, will create such a panic, fury, and despair as could only be compared with the mass psychosis resulting from the Black Death in the Middle Ages. The traumatic effects of such a catastrophe would lead to a new form of primitive barbarism, to the resurgence of the most archaic elements, which are still potentialities in every man and of which we have had ample evidence in the terror systems of Hitler and Stalin. It would sound most unlikely to many students of human nature and psychopathology that human beings could cherish freedom, respect for life or love after having witnessed and participated in the unlimited cruelty of man against man which thermonuclear war would mean. It is a psychological fact that acts of brutality have a brutalizing effect on the participants and lead to more brutality.

But What If the Deterrent Works?

What is the likely future of the social character of man in a bilateral or multilateral armed world, where, no matter how complex the problems or how full the satisfactions of any particular society, the biggest and most pervasive reality in any man's life is the poised missile, the humming data processor connected to it, the waiting radiation counters and seismographs, the overall technocratic perfection (overlying the nagging but impotent fear of its imperfection) of the mechanism of holocaust? To live for any length of time under the constant threat of destruction creates certain psychological effects in most human beings—fright, hostility, callousness, a hardening of the heart, and a resulting indifference to all the values we cherish. Such conditions will transform us into barbarians—though barbarians equipped with the most complicated machines. If we are serious in claiming that our aim is to preserve freedom (that is, to prevent the subordination of the individual under an all-powerful state), we must admit that this freedom will be lost, whether the deterrent works or does not work.

Aside from these psychological facts, the continuation of the arms race constitutes a particular threat to Western culture.[7] In the process of conquering nature, producing and consuming have become Western man's main preoccupation—the goal of his life. We have transformed means into ends. We manufacture machines which are like men, and we produce men who are like machines. In his work, the individual is managed as a part of a production team. During his leisure time, he is manipulated as a consumer who likes what he is told to like and yet has the illusion that he follows his own taste. In centering his life around the production of things, man himself is in danger of becoming a thing, worshiping the idols of the production machine and the state while he is under the illusion of worshiping God. "Things are in the saddle and ride mankind," as Emerson has put it. Circumstances which we created have consolidated themselves into powers which rule over us. The technical and bureaucratic system we have built tells us what to do, it decides for us. We may not be in danger of becoming slaves, but we are in danger of becoming robots, and the human values of our tradition are threatened—integrity, individuality, responsibility, reason, and love. Talking about these values more and more becomes an empty ritual.

This trend toward a world of impotent men directed by virile machines (both in the United States and in the Soviet Union)—brought about by technological and demographic factors, and by the increasing centralization and bureaucracy in big corporations and government—will reach the point of no return if we continue the arms race. Dangerous as our present situation is, we still have a chance to put man back into the saddle, to effect a renaissance of the spiritual values of the great humanistic tradition. Unless such a renaissance occurs, unless we can achieve a radical revitalization of the spirit on which our culture is founded, we shall lose the vitality necessary for survival and we shall decay, just as many other great powers have decayed in history. The real threat to our existence is not communist ideology, it is not even the communist military power—it is the hollowness of our beliefs, the fact that freedom, individuality, and faith have become empty formulas, that God has become an idol, that our vitality is sapped because we have no vision except that of having more of the same. It seems that a great deal of the hatred of communism is, in the last analysis, based on a deep disbelief in the spiritual values of democracy. Hence, instead of experiencing love of what we are *for*, we experience hate of what we are *against*. If we continue to live in fear of extinction and to plan mass destruction of others, the last chance for a revival of our humanist-spiritual tradition will be lost.

Benefits and Dangers of Unilateral Disarmament

If these are the dangers of the policy of the deterrent, what do the proponents of unilateral disarmament consider to be the benefits—and the dangers—of their policy?

The most likely result of unilateral disarmament—whether it be undertaken by the United States or by the Soviet Union—is that it would prevent war. The main reason which could impel either the Soviet Union or the United States to atomic war is the constant fear of being attacked and pulverized by the opponent. This position is succinctly expressed by Herman Kahn, who is in no way a proponent of unilateral disarmament. Kahn states that, "aside from the ideological differences and the problem of security itself, there does not seem to be any objective quarrel between the United States and Russia that justifies the risks and costs that we subject each other to. The big thing that the Soviet Union and the United States have to fear from each other is fear itself.[8] If, indeed, the main cause of war lies in mutual fear, then the disarmament of either the Soviet Union or the United States would most likely do away with this major cause and, thus, with the probability of war.

But are there motives other than fear which could prompt the Soviet Union to try for world conquest? One such motive could be economic interest in expansion, which was a basic motivation for the initiation of war in the nineteenth century and also for the first two world wars. Exactly here we see the difference between the nature of the conflicts in 1914 or 1939 and the present situation. In World War I, Germany threatened British markets and the French sources of coal and iron; in 1939, Hitler needed territorial conquest for the economic expansion he wanted. Today, neither the Soviet Union nor the United States has overriding economic interests in the conquest of markets and supplies, since a 2 or 3 percent rise in the level of national productivity would bring a greater advantage than would any military conquest, and, moreover, each has the capital, raw material, supplies, and population for a constant increase in its general productivity.[9]

The more serious possible motive is found in the fear, widely held in the United States, that the Soviet Union is out to conquer the world for communism and that, if the United States disarmed, Russia would be all the more eager to achieve her wish for world domination. This idea of Russian intentions is based on an erroneous appreciation of the nature of the present-day Soviet Union. It is true that under Lenin and Trotsky the Russian Revolution was aimed at conquering the capitalistic world (or at least, Europe) for communism, partly because the communist leaders were convinced that there was no possibility of success for communist Russia unless the highly industrialized states of Europe (or at least Germany) joined their system, and partly because they were prompted by the belief that the victory of the communist revolution in the world would bring about the fulfillment of their secular-messianic hopes.

The failure of these hopes and the ensuing victory of Stalin brought about a complete change in the nature of Soviet communism. The annihilation of almost all the old Bolsheviks was only a symbolic act for the destruction of the old revolutionary idea. Stalin's slogan of "socialism in one country" covered one simple aim—the rapid industrialization of Russia, which the Czarist system had not accomplished. Russia repeated the same process of accumulating capital which Western capitalism had gone through in the eighteenth and nineteenth centuries. The essential difference is that, while in these centuries in the West the sanctions were purely economic, the Stalinist system now developed political sanctions of direct terror; in addition, it employed socialist ideology to sugar-coat the exploitation of the masses. The Stalinist system was neither a socialist nor a revolutionary system, but a state-capitalism based on ruthless methods of planning and economic centralization.

The period of Khrushchevism is characterized by the fact that capital accumulation has succeeded to a point where the population can enjoy a great deal more consumption and is less forced to make sacrifices; as a result, the political terror can be greatly reduced.

But Khrushchevism has by no means changed the basic character of Soviet society in one essential respect: it is not a revolutionary nor a socialist regime, but one of the most conservative, class-ridden regimes anywhere in the Western world, humanly coercive, economically effective. While the aim of democratic socialism was the emancipation of man, the overcoming of his alienation, and the eventual abolition of the state, the "socialist" slogans used in Soviet Russia reflect empty ideologies, and the social reality is the very opposite of true socialism. The ruling class of the Soviet Union is no more revolutionary than the Renaissance popes were followers of the teachings of Christ. To try to explain Khrushchev by quoting Marx, Lenin, or Trotzky shows an utter failure to understand the historical development which has taken place in the Soviet Union and an incapacity to appreciate the difference between facts and ideologies. It should be added that our attitude is the best propaganda service the Russians could wish for. Against the facts, they try to convince the workers of Western Europe and the peasants in Asia that they represent the ideas of socialism, of a classless society, etc. The Western attitude, of falling for this propaganda, does exactly what the Russians want: to confirm these claims. (Unfortunately very few people except democratic socialists have sufficient knowledge of the difference between socialism and its distorted and corrupt form which calls itself Soviet socialism.)

The role of Russia is still more emphasized by the fact that Russia feels threatened by a potentially expansionist China. Russia one day might be in the same position with regard to China as we believe we are in relation to Russia. If the threat to Russia from the United States were to disappear, Russia could devote her energy to coping with the threat from China, unless by universal disarmament this threat would cease to exist.

The above-mentioned considerations indicate that the dangers which might arise if the Soviet Union were not to give up its armaments are more remote than they seem to many. Would the Soviet Union use her military superiority to try to occupy the United States or Western Europe? Aside from the fact that it would be exceedingly difficult, to say the least, for the Soviet Union's agents to run the economic and political machines of the United States or Western Europe, and aside from the fact that there is no vital need for Russia to conquer these territories, it would be most inconvenient to try to do so—and for a reason which is generally not sufficiently appreciated. Even the procommunist workers in the West have no idea of the degree of coercion to which they would have to submit under a Soviet system. They, as well as noncommunist workers, would oppose the new authorities, who would be forced to use tanks and machine guns against the protesting workers. This would encourage revolutionary tendencies in the satellite states, or even within the Soviet Union, and be most undesirable to the Soviet rulers; it would especially endanger Khrushchev's policy of liberalization, and hence his whole political position.

Eventually the Soviet Union might try to exploit its military superiority for the penetration of Asia and Africa. This is possible, but, with our present policy of the deterrent, it is doubtful whether the United States would really be willing to start a thermonuclear war in order to prevent the Russians from gaining certain advantages in the world outside of Europe and the Americas.

All these assumptions may be wrong. The position of the proponents of unilateral disarmament is that the chance that they are wrong is much smaller than the chance that the continuation of the arms race will finish civilization as we cherish it.

Some Psychological Considerations

One cannot discuss the question of what might happen as a result of unilateral disarmament—or, for that matter, of any mutual disarmament—without examining some psychological arguments. The most popular one is that "the Russians cannot be trusted." If "trust" is meant in a moral sense, it is unfortunately true that political leaders can rarely be trusted. The reason lies in the split between private and public morals: the state, having become an idol, justifies any immorality if committed in its interest, while the very same political leaders would not commit the same acts if they were acting in behalf of their own private interests. However, there is another meaning to "trust in people," a meaning which is much more relevant to the problem of politics: the trust that they are sane and rational beings, and that they will act accordingly. If I deal with an opponent in whose sanity I trust, I can appreciate his motivations and to some extent predict them, because there are certain rules and aims, like that of survival or that of commensurateness between aims and means, which are common to all sane people. Hitler could not be trusted because he was lacking in sanity, and this very lack destroyed both him and his regime. It seems quite clear that the Russian leaders of today are sane and rational people; therefore, it is important not only to know what they are capable of, but also to predict what they might be motivated to do.[10]

This question of the leaders' and the people's sanity leads to another consideration which affects us as much as it does the Russians. In the current discussion on armament control, many arguments are based on the question of what is *possible*, rather than on what is *probable*. The difference between these two modes of thinking is precisely the difference between *paranoid* and *sane* thinking. The paranoiac's unshakable conviction in the validity of his delusion rests upon the fact that it is logically possible, and, so, unassailable. It is logically possible that his wife, children, and colleagues hate him and are conspiring to kill him. The patient cannot be convinced that his delusion is *impossible;* he can only be told that it is exceedingly *unlikely*. While the latter position requires an examination and evaluation of the facts and also a certain amount of faith in life, the paranoid position can satisfy itself with the possibility alone. I submit that our political thinking suffers from such paranoid trends. We should be concerned, not with the possibilities, but rather with the probabilities. This is the only sane and realistic way of conducting the affairs of national as well as of individual life.

Again on the psychological plane, there are certain misunderstandings of the radical disarmament position which occur in many of the discussions. First of all, the position of unilateral disarmament has been understood as one of submission and resignation. On the contrary, the pacifists as well as the humanist pragmatists believe that unilateral disarmament is possible only as an expression of a deep spiritual and moral change within ourselves: it is an act of courage and resistance—not one of cowardice or surrender. Forms of resistance differ in accordance with the respective viewpoints. On the other hand, Gandhists and men like King-Hall advocate nonviolent resistance, which undoubtedly requires the maximum of courage and faith; they refer to the example of Indian resistance against Britain or Norwegian resistance against the Nazis. This point of view is succinctly expressed in *Speak Truth to Power* (see reference 4):

> Thus, we dissociate ourselves from the basically selfish attitude that has been miscalled pacifism, but that might be more accurately described as a kind of irresponsible antimilitarism. We dissociate ourselves also from utopianism. Though the choice of nonviolence involves a radical change in men, it does not require perfection. . . . We have tried to make it clear that readiness to accept suffering—rather than inflict it on others—is the essence of the nonviolent life, and that we must be prepared if called upon to pay the ultimate price. Obviously, if men are willing to spend billions of treasure and countless lives in war, they cannot dismiss the case for nonviolence by saying that in a nonviolent struggle people might be killed! It is equally clear that where commitment and the readiness to sacrifice are lacking, nonviolent resistance cannot be effective. On the contrary, it demands greater discipline, more arduous training, and more courage than its violent counterpart.[11]

Some think of armed resistance, of men and women defending their lives and their freedom with rifles, pistols, or knives. It is not unrealistic to think that both forms of resistance, nonviolent or violent, might deter an aggressor from attacking. At least, it is more realistic than to think that the use of thermonuclear weapons could lead to a "victory for democracy."

The proponents of "security by armament" sometimes accuse us of having an unrealistic, flatly optimistic picture of the nature of man. They remind us that this "perverse human being has a dark, illogical, irrational side."[12] They even go so far as to say that "the paradox of nuclear deterrence is a variant of the fundamental Christian paradox. In order to *live*, we must express our willingness to kill and to die."[13] Apart from this crude falsification of Christian teaching, we are by no means oblivious of the potential evil within man and of the tragic aspect of life. Indeed, there are situations in which man must be willing to die in order to live. In the sacrifices necessary for violent or nonviolent resistance, I can see an expression of the acceptance of tragedy and sacrifice. But, there is no tragedy or sacrifice in irresponsibility and carelessness; there is no meaning or dignity in the idea of the destruction of mankind and of civilization. Man has in himself a potential for evil; his whole existence is beset by dichotomies rooted in the very conditions of his existence. But these truly tragic aspects must not be confused with the results of stupidity and lack of imagination, with the willingness to stake the future of mankind on a gamble.

Finally, to take up one last criticism, directed against the position of unilateral disarmament: that it is "soft" on communism. Our position is precisely based on the negation of the Soviet principle of the omnipotence of the state. Just because the spokesmen for unilateral disarmament are drastically opposed to the supremacy of the state, they do not want to grant the state the ever-increasing power which is unavoidable in the arms race, and they deny the right of the state to make decisions which can lead to the destruction of a great part of humanity and can doom future generations. If the basic conflict between the Soviet system and the democratic world is the question of the defense of the individual against the encroachment of an omnipotent state, then, indeed, the position for unilateral disarmament is the one which is most radically opposed to the Soviet principle.

After having discussed the case for unilateral disarmament (in the broad sense), I want to return to the practical proposition of unilateral steps toward disarmament. I do not deny that there are risks involved in this limited form of unilateral action, but considering the fact that the present method of negotiations has produced no results and that the chances that they will in the future are rather slim, considering furthermore the grave risk involved in the continuation of the arms race, I believe that it is practically and morally justified to take this risk. At present we are caught in a position with little chance for survival, unless we want to take refuge in hopes. *If* we have enough shelters, *if* there is enough time for a warning and strategic evacuation of cities, *if* the "United States' active offenses and active defenses can gain control of the military situation after only a few exchanges," [14] we might have only five, or twenty-five, or seventy million killed. However, if these conditions do not materialize, "an enemy could, by repeated strikes, reach almost any level of death and destruction he wished." [15] (And, I assume, the same threat exists for the Soviet Union.) In such a situation, "when nations are poised at the last moment when an agreement appears possible to end the risk of horrifying war, unleashed by fanatics, lunatics or men of ambition," [16] it is imperative to shake off the inertia of our accustomed thinking, to seek for new approaches to the problem, and above all, to see new alternatives to the present choices that confront us.

Notes

1. Charles E. Osgood's "Suggestions for Winning the Real War with Communism," "Conflict Resolution," vol. III, no. 4, December 1959, p. 131, and also "A Case for Graduated Unilateral Disarmament," *Bulletin of Atomic Scientists*, vol. XVI, no. 4, pp. 127 ff.

2. This condition is in my opinion to be taken only as an optimal *desideratum*, since any weakening of one power's aggressive potential means strategically some increase in the opponent's aggressive potential.

3. Charles E. Osgood's "Suggestions for Winning the Real War with Communism," p. 316.

4. Bertrand Russell, *Common Sense and Nuclear Warfare*. London: G. Allen & Unwin, Ltd., 1959. Stephen King-Hall, *Defense in the*

Nuclear Age. Nyack, N.Y.: Fellowship Publications, 1959. Jerome Davis and H. B. Hester, *On the Brink.* New York: Lyle Stuart, 1959. Lewis Mumford, *The Human Way Out.* Pendell Hill Pamphlet no. 97, 1958. C. W. Mills, *The Causes of World War Three.* New York: Seeker & Warburg, 1959. George F. Kennan, "Foreign Policy and Christian Conscience," *The Atlantic Monthly,* May 1959. Richard B. Gregg, *The Power of Nonviolence.* Nyack, N.Y.: Fellowship Publications, 1959. American Friends Service Committee, *Speak Truth to Power, Quaker Search for an Alternative to Balance.* 1955.

5. George F. Kennan, *loc. cit.* pp. 44 ff.

6. This premise is shared by the report of the National Planning Association of America: *1970 Without Arms Control; Implications of Modern Weapons Technology* (by NPA Special Project Committee on Security through Arms Control; Planning Pamphlet no. 104, May 1958, Washington, D.C.), which states: "Not only does the danger of war remain a possibility, but the probability totalled over time increases, becoming a certainty if sufficient time elapses without succeeding in finding alternatives." Or, E. Finley Carter, President of the Stanford Research Institute, writes: "In the search for security through the application of technology to weapons for destruction, the Soviet bloc and the Western allies have created a mortal common enemy—the threat of accidental nuclear war" (*SRI Journal,* Stanford Research Institute, Fourth Quarter, 1959, vol. 3, p. 198). Herman Kahn also concludes, "It is most unlikely that the world can live with an uncontrolled arms race lasting for several decades" (*ibid.,* p. 139). He emphasizes that it is unrealistic to believe that war has become impossible because of its extremely destructive character.

The advisor on Science and Technology of the Democratic Advisory Council of 27 December 1959 declared: "All-out nuclear war seems not only possible but probable as long as we pursue our present military policies and fail to achieve international agreements of broad scope designed to alleviate this unstable situation. The triggering of a nuclear war by mistake, by misadventure or by miscalculation is a constant danger." It must be stressed that the danger lies not only in technical errors, but equally in the blundering decision-making by political and military leaders. If one remembers the political and military blunders committed by many of the leaders in the conduct of wars of 1914 and 1939, it is not difficult to visualize that, given present-day weapons, the same type of leaders will blow the world to pieces, in spite of good intentions.

7. For a detailed analysis of modern society cf. my *The Sane Society.* New York: Holt, Rinehart and Winston, 1955.

8. *SRI Journal*, 1959, vol. 3, p. 140.

9. For the very same reasons, there is a real chance for the future abolition of war, a chance which never existed in the past. In most of man's history, the improvement of his material situation required an increase in human energy (slaves), additional land for cattle raising or agriculture, or new sources of raw materials. The techniques of the present and of the future will permit an increase in material wealth by an increased industrial and—indirectly—an agricultural productivity, without the need of enslaving or robbing others. At present and in the future, war would have as its only "rationale" the irrationality of human desire for power and conquest.

10. Whether or not political leaders are sane is not a matter of historical accident. Any government which has set out to do the impossible—for instance, to achieve equality and justice when the requisite material conditions are lacking—will produce fanatical and irrational leaders. This was the case with Robespierre, as it was with Stalin. Or, a government which tries to reconcile the interests of the most backward social class (the lower middle class) with those of the economically progressive classes (workers and businessmen) as the Nazi government did, again will produce fanatical and irrational leaders. The Soviet Union today is on the road toward solving its economic problems successfully; hence it is not surprising that her leaders are realistic men of common sense.

11. *Loc. cit.* p. 52 and p. 65.

12. Peter B. Young, "The Renunciationists," *Airpower*, the Air Force Historical Foundation, vol. VII, no. 1, p. 33.

13. *Ibid.*

14. Herman Kahn, *Report on a Study of Non-Military Defense.* Rand Corporation, 1958, p. 13.

15. *Ibid.*

16. General de Gaulle, in a speech in April 1960.

IX.   The Psychological Problems
of Aging

One of the first questions on the psychological problems of aging that we have to answer is: Is old age something embarrassing? Is it a painful stage on the way out which should be sugar-coated with all sorts of words, or is it just a stage of life like adolescence, like infancy, like middle age; is the problem not the same as it is with all stages of living, namely, how do we live well and how are we most alive in that particular stage?

One may meaningfully speak of an art of living and may therefore say that the art of aging is just as important a chapter—in the art of living—as the art of being a child and the art of being an adolescent.

Quite obviously, the whole problem of old age is a problem of modern industrial society. Old age was very rare one hundred years ago or even fifty years ago. To live to see one's grandchildren or one's great-grandchildren was a great exception then, while today it has become more and more frequent. It is quite clear that old age is a problem created by modern industrial society. It is primarily a problem of the progress in medicine which is only a part of the general progress in science and in technology.

Besides that, we might even say that old age can be defined not only in biological or physiological terms, but also in social terms: old age is a time when you don't have to work anymore. Now, when this time comes when you don't have to work anymore, is, to a large extent, a question of industrial organization. We can visualize that with increasing automation, not only work hours will be shortened, but the working age will be reduced more and more so that, perhaps fifty years from now, old age will be anything above forty because nobody will have to work or will have an opportunity to work—with the exception of a few people—after the age of forty.

Now we in Western society have not only prolonged life, we have been fortunate enough to have had the material means to make this prolonged life dignified, comfortable, and agreeable. We all know that a great part of the problem of overpopulation in the world is due to the fact that medicine has worked but industry has not or could not create the material means to benefit from what medicine has done. In such situations you have a population increase without the corresponding satisfaction of the material needs of the people who live longer. We, in the United States, and all industrial societies, in general, have the means, and have them more and more, so as not to have this contradiction.

Our modern industrial society has created a new age for man: old age. Now old age is something which man can live through securely and *could* live through happily if modern society had not also created some other phenomena which are not so good and which have a particular impact on the question of aging. I shall talk about some of these problems and try to link them up with the problems of aging.

Modern society creates a type of man whom I have earlier called the *homo consumens*—the consumer man whose main interest becomes, aside from working from nine to five, to consume.

This is the attitude of the eternal suckling. It is the attitude of the man or the woman with the open mouth who consumes everything with voracity—liquor, cigarettes, movies, television, lectures, books, art exhibits, sex; everything is transformed into an article of consumption.

Certainly, for those who sell all these articles, there is nothing wrong with this. They try to promote the consumer spirit as much as they can; but, if I may apply some knowledge of my own profession, there is something very deeply wrong with this, because we know that behind this urge to consume there is an inner vacuity—a sense of emptiness. There is, in fact, a sense of depression, a sense of loneliness. We find the clinical evidence for this connection in the fact that, very often, overeating and overbuying are the results of states of depression or intense anxiety. The person feels inwardly empty or helpless and by taking things in he gets a feeling that he fills himself with something which makes him strong.

Naturally, this is not a conscious thought process; it is too unreflective for that, but it is one of those unconscious experiences in which inner emptiness is compensated for by consumption—endless and unlimited consumption.

In fact, our concept of freedom, if we do not refer to the kind of freedom which is discussed in political terms, our real concept of freedom today is largely a concept of freedom to buy and to consume. In the nineteenth century, freedom meant, to a large extent, freedom of private property and freedom to do with my private property whatever I saw fit. Today, private property in our society is disappearing, relatively, in comparison with income from salaries. What we feel as freedom is, to a large extent, the freedom to buy or to consume; that is to say, to choose between many, many different things and to say: "I want this cigarette. I want this car. I want this thing rather than another." Precisely because many of the competing brands are not in reality very different, the individual feels the great power of being free to choose. I think many people, if they were honest with their concept of heaven, would imagine heaven to be a tremendous department store in which they could buy something new every day and perhaps a little more than their neighbors.

There is a certain sickness in this drive for ever-increasing consumption and the danger is that, by being filled with a need for consumption, the person does not really solve the problem of inner passivity, of inner vacuity, of anxiety, of being depressed—because life in some way doesn't make sense.

The Old Testament warns that the worst sin of the Hebrews was that they had lived without joy in the midst of plenty. I am afraid the critics of our society could also say that we live with much fun and excitement but with little joy in the midst of plenty.

I am discussing this in connection with the problems of the aging for the simple reason that I fear there is great danger that the aged might become *super-consumers*. They might become the people who have time not only to consume from nine to five, but who also have time to consume from nine to twelve and make consumption their main business. They might become people who are treated with a certain condescension by the young, and who now can become completely indolent and spend their time in *killing time*.

It is our peculiar characteristic to make so much effort at saving time, and when we have saved time we are embarrassed because we don't know what to do with it. Then we start to kill time. Our amusement industry shows us how to kill time without knowing it, by having us consume amusements with the conscious conviction that what we are doing makes some sense. It seems to me that there is a certain danger that we may transform the aging, with all the possibilities they have, with all this free time, into that super-consumer who is completely passive and kills time in what the experts would call *a decent way*. That, I think, would be a great shame.

The fact is that old age is a great challenge and a great

chance. It could be the best time a man ever had because he is freed from the task of making a living, he is freed from the anxieties of losing a job, he is freed from the need to please a superior in order to be promoted; he is really a free man—almost as free as we are in our sleep when we are, as our dreams show, so much more creative than we ever thought we could be.

The older person, let us say after sixty-five, really has a chance to live, to be alive, to make living his main business. He can also confront himself genuinely with the spiritual and religious problems of life. I think that in the past history of humanity men usually had no energy or no time left to be seriously concerned with such problems.

If you are a manual worker, you are too tired, and if you are not a manual worker then your ambitions and your doubts about your success make you too tired to really think much about the problems of life. We talk occasionally, usually on Sundays, about them: What is the meaning of life? Who am I? What is my place in the world? What reason or purpose has all this living and activity? These are the problems that one might listen to in a sermon on Sundays, but usually on weekdays one has neither the time nor the energy to think about such matters.

In the coming age of automation, when people eventually might work only ten or twenty hours a week, man, for the first time, will be forced to confront himself with the true spiritual problems of living.

The aged have a chance to confront themselves with it right now, to raise these questions, not just as a theory, but as something which concerns them. Who am I? What is my aim in life? What is life about anyway? They have a chance to confront themselves with the question which is part of the philosophy of life, the question of death—the ultimate reality nobody escapes—and to view life under the perspective that it ends with death.

If I say life ends with death I express something which Christians or Jews who believe in a world after life will not accept. However, I think they would agree with me in one thing: even if one believes in life after death it is certainly not a prepaid guided tour in a very foreign country. It is no pleasure trip. It is there only if something happens in our life *here* which makes it possible to participate in that kind of life which various religious systems describe. It doesn't really matter too much whether we do or do not believe in certain religious statements or dogmas about life after death, for it would still mean we have to take this problem of death seriously and not try to camouflage it or to run away from it.

I have examined the question of taking certain fundamental problems of life seriously and I shall now consider how this question might be answered. What is the opposite of the consumer? What is the opposite of the empty, passive person who spends—or as I would say, *wastes*—his life by killing time?

This is very difficult to describe, but I would say, in a general way, the main answer is *to be interested*. Unfortunately, we use this word so often that it has lost a great deal of its meaning, the meaning being how its root is defined in Latin: *inter-esse*, "to be in" something; that is to say, to be able to transcend one's ego, to leave the narrow confines of my ego with all my ambitions, with my pride of property, with my pride of what I know and my family and my wife and my husband and my and my and my. It means to forget all these things and to reach out to both that which is opposite me and that which is in front of me, whether that is a child or a flower or a book or an idea or man or whatever it may be.

Interest means to be active, but to be active in the sense of Aristotle or in the sense of Spinoza, and not to be active in the sense of modern *busy-ness* where one must do something all the time. Any person who can sit for an hour or two and do nothing is probably more active, in this sense, than most of us are when we are doing something all the time; it is, of course, much more difficult. It is a real problem for the older person to be capable of being active in this inner sense rather than in the outer sense.

The problem of false activity cannot be ignored. It is not only in the spheres of busy-ness, but also in another sphere in which people often deceive themselves about the activity of their feelings. An example which, perhaps, sounds far-fetched, but which I believe is related to the problem must be emphasized: Mr. A. is being hypnotized. Let us assume that it is 9:00 A.M. He is told by the hypnotist that this afternoon, at 3:00 P.M., he will take off his coat and, unless some other suggestions are given, he will forget that this happened. Now let us assume that you meet Mr. A. at 2:30. You talk with him about the weather, about politics, whatever you are interested in at the moment. At just a minute before 3:00 P.M., Mr. A. will say: "Isn't it an awfully hot day? Really, I have to take off my coat."

Now, if it's really a warm day you will think this is very sensible, or if it's a very cold day but the heating is so hot that you can't stand it, you will still think that his reaction is very sensible. However, if it's a day which is not too hot and your building is not overheated, you will be very surprised that Mr. A. feels it is so hot, and you might think he is running a fever and suggest that he go to the doctor. Nonetheless, you are convinced that Mr. A. feels hot and has a need to take off his coat. If, however, you had been present at 9:00 A.M. during the hypnotic session, you would know that this whole feeling of being hot was only induced by the suggestion of the hypnotist. Still, there is this interesting phenomenon that Mr. A. has the need to make what he does appear rational. Mr. A. cannot simply, spontaneously take off his coat. No, he has to find a reason for it. If you were not present in the morning you would be convinced that he really feels warm.

This is only a special case of what happens many times, even without hypnosis. We believe we feel something which we really do not feel, simply because we follow suggestions, public opinion, and the like. Then we have to find a reason for these actions which seem to be motivated by the feeling—we rationalize. For example, if you belong to a cultural elite, you probably feel that Pablo Picasso's work is very beautiful and constitutes great art. However, if you are indoctrinated that Picasso has created something beautiful, you look at the paintings and feel that they are wonderful, but you *feel* nothing really. All that happens is that you have a *thought of feeling* something, and most people are not quite able to differentiate or distinguish between a genuine feeling—which is a reality, which corresponds to something that goes on in the whole physiological system of the person—and the thought of a feeling, which is almost like a real feeling, except that it isn't.

If a person tries to observe in the only laboratory he has within himself, that is, his own life, he will find that often he has a conviction that he feels something—interest, love, joy, or other emotions—when actually he has only thoughts about feelings.

However, there are many occasions when one's feelings are pseudo-feelings; one feels as he is supposed to feel by indoctrination of the culture; there are many situations where one feels what he is supposed to feel and cannot know the difference between authentic feelings and pseudo-feelings, which are, in reality, nothing but a thought.

Now these pseudo-feelings are something quite different from real interest, from active participation, from reaching out. If life is to be interesting, one has to be interested, otherwise life is boring, and in despair one will reach out for all sorts of means to dispel this boredom. Despite the fact that there is so much talk about the unconscious—and usually people think about the Oedipus complex, incestuous wishes and all of those kinds of things—I think there is probably nothing more repressed than the feeling of boredom people have.

Unconscious boredom in modern culture has tremendous

proportions and the success of radio and television and similar articles of consumption is only possible because people are so emptied of genuine experiences. In our society we are indoctrinated to believe that to be disinterested is quite indecent, or at least it is significant of failure; the "successful" person is interested in something. Because of this, we have to replace the sense of boredom with a sense of excitement, although actually this excitement is often nothing but a thought motivated by the indoctrination that certain situations or persons are supposed to be exciting.

It is easy to make the connection between what I have been saying about interest and boredom and the problems of old people who have nothing to be busy with and who have lots of time.

Another psychological aspect of aging is the fact that very often the real character of a person appears more truly in old age than it did at the time when he was occupied, had to be pleasant, had to find jobs, and had to keep jobs. Sometimes people think an aging person automatically deteriorates. But there is not necessarily any deterioration. Until now he had to present the appearance of being vital because it was necessary; but when it was not necessary, he really revealed the deterioration to which he had succumbed.

We all know that in our working life many, if not most of us, want to project what psychologists sometimes call a *persona*—we want to project a picture of ourselves which is best adapted to the particular kind of work we are doing. However, if one is a surgeon, and a very good surgeon, one does not have to present such an appearance because, in the first place, the patient hardly sees the surgeon and, in the second place, he is so happy to find a good surgeon that he is indifferent as to whether the surgeon smiles or not. If you are a skilled worker in a steel mill, it is not necessary to be very pleasant either, because all that matters is that you are skilled and that your coworkers can rely on you. Nonetheless, in most occupations and professions today, in our bureacratically organized society, it is very important to be pleasant—sometimes even more important than to have skills. If you have both, of course, it is an asset, but the appearance of pleasantness is very important.

However, when you do not have to be pleasant anymore, why not be unpleasant? Why not at last feel: Now I can be myself! This is not to say that there are so many unpleasant people, but there are quite a few and it is wrong to attribute all disagreeableness found in older people to deterioration caused by old age. In fact, for the first time many of these older people are free to be themselves.

But this does not hold true only for the disagreeable people; it also holds true for very kind people. If you are very kind in business you are a simpleton; and you will be aware of this in the attitude people express in their relationship to you. As a result, you are really ashamed of the kindness of your heart, for even though you would wish to give some merchandise to someone who cannot afford to buy it, you find that you have to repress this feeling—you must not even be aware of it—because if you do that, even if you can afford it, you have been indoctrinated to the extent that you would be considered a simpleton.

However, when you are old you may feel free to be your own true self in this positive sense, so you can become a kinder person than you were permitted to be in certain social situations in the past.

What I mean to say is that, for better or worse, the older person has a chance—and very often uses that chance—to permit himself to live according to his true character rather than according to that fancied character which he assumed when he needed to get ahead.

Therefore, in any attempt to arrive at an understanding of old people, I think that an understanding of various forms of character structures is quite important—just as important as it is for an understanding of younger people. I would suggest that a study of old people should be concerned with the study of character structure and of the differences in character. One great difference in character between people is found in those who *love life* and all that is alive, and those who, in a perverse way, *love death*—are attracted by decay, by all that is unalive.

I have written about this in some detail in *The Heart of Man*, and I will mention here, only briefly, the essential point which I was trying to make. Most people believe that all men love life. Unfortunately, this is not so. There is a minority who are really more attracted by decay—by all that is mechanical, by all that is not alive—than by all that is alive. I have used the words *necrophilia* and *biophilia*, the love of the dead and the love of life, in differentiating the two groups.

You can sometimes see an example of the necrophilous type in a mother, for instance, who comes to life when she talks about the illnesses of her child. If her child has enjoyed something and comes home full of *aliveness*, that mother will hardly notice, but when the child is sick, then she really will be interested. You might even excuse this behavior because there is some reason at least for a mother to be interested in her child's health. However, you will find many people who are most interested in burials, in death, in sickness, whose favorite conversation is the history of their sicknesses, and you can see that for older people this could easily become much more of a rationalized preoccupation than for younger people.

As we get older, we all begin to study medicine; we have one sickness and then another and soon we become specialists in various fields—but hopefully, not in too many. Now the necrophilous person, when he sees that he has perhaps only ten or fifteen years to live and death becomes very close to his heart, he finds that he does not have to repress his necrophilous tendencies anymore. He can now, overtly, be concerned with sickness and death and he becomes not only a bore, but a real danger for all who live around him because he spreads an atmosphere of gloom gleefully. For him, of course, it isn't really gloom; for him, it's the most exciting thing in the world—to think about sickness and death—but for people who love life, it's terrible.

Now, if you don't know that you are dealing with what you might call, in a broad sense, a sickness, then you might easily find yourself caught in this atmosphere of gloom —particularly if you feel a compassion for this person who cannot stop talking about illness.

I think if one does care for the aged, one should be very aware that this preoccupation with sickness, death and burials is not at all just a natural outcome of being old. Most of the time it is the more frank expression or manifestation of a tendency these people have had all their lives; namely, to get excited about the one thing which one should not get excited about—decay.

Another psychological attitude which is relevant for the aging has to do with the difference between *independence* and *dependence*. All of us are independent. We all have jobs and we no longer accept money from our parents. We are also dependent: we are dependent on our employers, on public opinion or, in the case of doctors, on the pleasure of their patients. Still, we feel independent if we earn our own money in some way or another.

Unfortunately, independence or freedom is not as easily achieved as it sounds. One of the basic problems of individual development is the problem which one might call, in psychological language, the problem of individuation: how does a person succeed in developing from a fetus in the womb into an independent person?

This is, of course, a long process. Obviously, as long as we are in the womb of our mothers we are not independent, in a very obvious physiological sense. Now when we are born, we are independent, physiologically, but we are not independent, psychologically. In fact, our existence in the first few weeks after birth may be in some way closer to our fetal life than our adult life. We are completely dependent on mother. We do not recognize her as a different person. We are, as I would call it, symbiotically related to mother. There is not yet a difference between the *me* and the *not me*. The whole world for the baby is *me*, and if any mother expects love from her four-week-old child, she lives with an illusion. In fact, if she expects much love from her one-year-old child, she is also a little bit misguided and headed for trouble.

The process of becoming *I*, a separate person who is related to the world, who is interested in the world, but who is independent, who owes his existence to himself, is one of the basic forms of human development.

Very sick people never go beyond the first symbiotic stage. A certain type of this psychotic person is one who emotionally and effectively still wants to live in his mother's womb, still wants to be symbiotically connected with mother or a person who takes her place.

Now you will find people who reach the stage where they only want to suck from mother's breasts; or others, somewhat further advanced, to sit on mother's lap; and still others, even a little more advanced, who wish only to be held by mother's or father's hand. Now only if a person reaches his full maturity will he be really on his own, that is to say, will he be able to stand on his own legs because he is actually related to the world, because he is connected with the world, not by being part of another person, but by his interest and love for the outside world. He can be truly independent because he is related; but most people don't reach this stage.

You find many people who do very well socially and economically, yet are not independent. This lack of independence is not visible on the surface, because they have a position which seems to be very independent. This is the case of many businessmen or professional persons who depend on their secretaries, wives, or public opinion, and yet, consciously feel that they are indeed independent.

I want to emphasize the relevance of the characterological trait for the aged, because very often it appears, as in the first case of necrophilia-biophilia, that an older person shows great signs of dependency and people think that it is simply due to aging when, in fact, this person has always been a dependent type and only now can afford to express it since, as an old person, he is supposed to be somewhat dependent. Here you see that whole psychology of a certain type of old people who feel like invalids, or who feel they need somebody to protect them. Old age, as we see it in our culture, gives them an excellent opportunity and rationalization to act out the dependency they had when they were thirty or forty, only at that time it was unconscious and concealed; but now they have an opportunity to manifest all their dependency.

Again, the problem here is not to succumb to this, but rather to see it for what it is; namely, a character trait which has always been present and which must now be counteracted, or perhaps even cured, but not be taken as a sign of old age.

There are other important character traits and character differences which sometimes reveal themselves in old age. For instance, one person might display envy. As long as he was younger, went ahead, was active, his envy was somewhat controlled or even repressed, because it did not create a good impression for him to indicate that he was envious. In fact, he had to conceal it if he wanted to get ahead, let us say, as a junior executive. He had to appear rather the opposite of being envious.

However, when this same person gets old, this envy that was always present will really become apparent—and it also has more to feed on. Such a person can now be envious of younger people, or even of older people who might not have had a severe illness. Now, again, the problem here is not to be deceived by the appearance of envy which develops because someone is old, but rather to know that this character trait exists now because it has a chance to manifest itself consciously and to be acted out. The person is the same as he always was.

Now you might wonder, even if I am right in my psychological description, what can be done about it. In the first place, I think that even the recognition that many characterological manifestations which are supposed to be manifestations of age, but which are really manifestations of character traits which were hidden but always present, is a help in one's response and reaction to these character traits. Secondly, I would say it might not even be too late for a person over sixty-five to change. The degree or the possibility to which a person can change does not primarily depend on age. It depends on his vitality, the intensity of his wish to change, on his interest, and many other factors.

There are young people of twenty-one, of whom one could say, without trying to be omniscient, that they will never change because there is some ingredient lacking, and whether they are twenty or thirty it will be always the same, they will remain the same inept persons throughout life. I have seen people of seventy who have changed their whole lives because, when seventy, they still had a great vitality and, in fact, at that age they found they finally had the first opportunity to really make changes and to consider who they wanted to be. I don't believe that old age, in itself, is necessarily a factor which precludes basic changes in character.

What I am saying here is that one should not be deceived by certain characterological traits which appear as a result of aging when, in fact, they have always been a part of the person; but also, one should not be unnecessarily skeptical that an old person can change, provided he has the will, the energy, the vitality and courage.

What we should avoid, however, as I mentioned earlier, is transforming the old person into the total consumer, making him into a person whom we teach how to pass away the time decently while he waits for his own passing—death. We should, therefore, have no condescension whatsoever about the old person, at least no more or no less than we might have about a young person. I don't think condescension is legitimate anywhere. You might have compassion, if a person has failed in his life and has no way of remedying this failure, but we might have compassion with many people of thirty and forty, of whom we can already say that they will fail in their lives and there will be no remedy for them.

This is not a problem of old age; this is a problem of human existence with each one of us. I believe that it is very important to think more about the problem of how we can help the older person to feel more active and more interested and to avoid the passive consumer life which is so often offered to him.

I know that there is still a great deal of research that must be done in this field, just as in education, in general. In fact, the two are not very different. How can you change a young student who only consumes lectures into a person who is actively interested in what he is studying? The same problem exists for the older person. How can you help to make him more alive than he has ever been, rather than feeling less alive? I think research in this field would be very helpful. How do you arouse a more active interest? Is it done by discussion, by reading, by a new interest in art or even a new interest in politics? When I refer to politics, I don't mean politics in the sense of reading whatever newspaper you read and then thinking what you have read is fine, but by waking up, making judgments, looking at events critically and seeing reality, and feeling responsible, that is to say, responding to what goes on, responding as a human being to what is taking place.

To sum up, the older person, like the younger, should try to become more responsive to the world around him; and to be responsive is the same as being responsible, both words deriving from the root, *respondere* (to respond). The older person must learn how *recreation* can become *re-creation*—a new capacity to be creative—and for this he does not need to be a painter or a poet or have any profession; all he needs to be is alive and that means to be truly and generally interested in the world.